RHYMES OF AN ASPIRING WRITER

A collection of my best poetry

Semisi Pone

BSc, MSc (Hons) Auckland

This book of poetry was compiled to commemorate the Third Anniversary of the Project Revival Charity Trust (Inc). It is a promotion of its charitable purpose of education in the community of Northcote Central, Northshore, Auckland, New Zealand.
18 June, 2016
Book and Art Exhibition
Methodist Hall,
Corner of Stafford Road and Queens Road,
 Northcote Point, Northshore
Auckland, New Zealand.

Introduction

This book of poetry is a collection of the best poetry I have written to date from my published books. They include 'Rhymes of an Aspiring Writer 1, 2 and 3', 'Green Earth. A Poetic Tree', 'Imagin' and 'The Loving Woman'.

The inspiration for these poems came from my love of poetry by the old masters such as R. L. Stevenson, S.T. Coleridge, Lord Byron, W. Wordsworth, J. Keats, Sir Walter Scott and others I read in High School.

I have always wanted to write some verses and the opportunity arose 5 years ago when I was between jobs and I decided to become a writer. I enjoyed literature and I have read many of the popular 'old' works such as Mark Twain, Robert Louis Stevenson and John Steinbeck novels. My favorites being 'Treasure Island' by R.L. Stevenson and 'Tom Sawyer' by Mark Twain.

Although writing has become an unprofitable profession for most writers in modern times, I believe that writing and producing books has far more value than just a commercial venture.

This collection commemorate the third anniversary of our Trust which is trying to help our youth with their education through promotion of reading.

I am hoping that this book like the 60 copies of THE DREAMTIME STORIES we gave away, to kids in Northcote, as Christmas presents last year (2015) will inspire our youth to do better at school.

We would like to see Teachers, Scientists, Lawyers, Doctors, Engineers, Writers and other professionals emerge from our kids in our Northcote Community in the future.

Writing will always be a key in furthering education. Books have become the most important resource in education anywhere in the world. Poetry is among the most loved of all genera and I hope you enjoy reading this book.

The poems are listed according to subject matter. They were written according to how I feel rather than what other writers do. I hope you will find some gems there for yourself.

Enjoy!

TABLE OF CONTENTS.

POEMS ABOUT;

1. POEMS ABOUT FAMILY

ARISTOTLE

He was a philosopher in ancient times
His story unfolds in a legend
A master of philosophy and arithmetic
Provides a scientific answer to every trick

He was a billionaire
With millions of shares
He asked Jackie Kennedy
To join his family

He is a little boy
Who gave us so much joy
His smile light up the world
And put our lives in a whirl

We hope he'll be wise and rich
Master the universe without a hitch
They will write songs in the future
His mind worked like a computer.

GIDEON

He laughs when he sees his sister
Then he crawls a bit quicker
'Cos he enjoy, just like a toy
Playing, he is a boy

He is only eight months old
But he is very bold
Just like Joshua of old
His mirth can crash Jericho

He enjoys riding in the car
He sits in the seat like a star
Then he blinks and fall asleep
Yawning, snoring just as quick

He looks up to his mummy
His mouth holding the dummy
Questioning as if to ask
Am I first in class?

He likes to have breakfast
First and not last
And jumps with glee
When he joins the family

He has cornflakes and nutragrain
To help him grow his brain
And eat his food like a main
While he peers at his gran

He looks around the table
Sister, nana, papa and uncle
They all look at him with pride
At the little boy by their side

Everyone hopes my grandson will grow
And learn the highs and the lows
And become a good man
Who will always like to learn.

MY CHILDREN

He cries in the middle of the night
I turned on the light
He wasn't happy
He soiled his nappy
I gave him a dry one
He is a lovely son
He gave us so much joy
My little boy

Then he got pushed aside
By somebody on the right

A little plumb, noisy girl
Whose smile light up the world
And always sleep in a curl
She is so boisterous and lovely
It amused the whole family

Then we got blessed again
With my current friend
Who is really smart
He worked out why cows fart
Just to make them go faster!
As he roared with laughter.

RHYMES FOR ALAYNA.

My granddaughter Alayna
Loves her Nana
She sleeps with her
She eats with her
She travels with her
In the car
With her Nana

My granddaughter Alayna
Loves her toys
She doesn't like the boys
Although they seek her attention
She's always filled with apprehension

She just wants a panda
Bought by her Nana

My granddaughter Alayna
Likes pasta
She takes a packet
And creates a racket
She wants the cook
To look in the book
With her Nana

My granddaughter Alayna
Is so cute
One day she will marry a Duke
We will travel to paradise
To have her wedding under the skies
A floating hotel boat
With her Nana

My granddaughter Alayna
Loves her brother
Little Gideon is her mate
He crawls through the gate
They play all the time
She keeps him in line
With her Nana.

MARLEY

She cries on the sofa
And laughs on my shoulder
Her sniffs and cold forgotten
No longer feeling rotten

My roots are spreading
To a farm in Huntly
A beautiful Maori girl
Now part of my world

A present from Maui
God of her Iwi
A bundle of joy
From my baby boy

Brisbane is her new home
On the Gold Coast
Learning the dreamtime
Aboriginal mime

Marley, soon you'll be two
This poem is for you
A present from grandpa
My pen is your waka

THE LOVE OF A FATHER

My children I leave you nothing but dust
  Dust that you must return to
  And dust that will be born
  Dust that will grow food for all
  For I am human and not of the Gods

My children I leave you nothing but words
  Words to keep in your memory
  And pass to your children
  Of how it was then, in our beginning
  And how it is now after we're born

My children I leave you nothing but hope
  Hope that you will one day join me
  Hope that you will continue our history
  Hope that you will understand my words
  When I was a man and did not understand

My children I leave you nothing but the stars
  The planets, the universe and everything you see
  For it was in my memory when I was a God
  And I passed it to you for our family
  That you can keep it for all and me.

ALAYNA

Her smile light up the sky
Seagull's feeding in the sunrise
Tuna feeding on a school of fry
Sparkles of silver in the sunlight

Shadows of grey
Disturb the glassy sea
Whish of waves in Gulliver's world
Her hair waving in the breeze

Crackle sounds of sand
A shining face in fairyland
Her tingling laughter disturb the birds
Doves awakening from their perch

Tangaroa[1] watched from the clouds
Maui[1] beckoned her to his boat
Let's go for a walkabout
A God in love with the Princess of Hearts.

---

1. Ancient Polynesian Gods

THE FUNERAL

A death in the family
Celebrating a life's passing
No faults remembered
Only the good qualities

Many who came never met
The deceased during life
But as relatives they feel
He is one of their own

Hymns and mass celebrated
As families remember their dead
Who they believe are in a better place
Their earthly lives a sinful game

They sing just like the angels sound
Imagination of the congregation
In Epsom's best cathedral
A father's sermon to match

A life, just like a flower
Fleeting as time itself
Lowered into the ground
In a golden, shiny casket

Their songs rise in the hot afternoon
Till we meet again, till we meet again
The talking chief gave the final speech
Of that dignified, crowded good-bye.

OUR LAND

My father gave me some land
It's my right under the constitution
A town allotment and farm
As investments in my future

I have done my share
Of work for the country
And still contribute hugely
In development and ideas

Now others claim my land is theirs
But I have the deeds to prove it
The government must stop them
Breeds of thieves for citizens

The King must do something
People must respect my rights
They should not steal from me
Inheritance for their children

A stolen property is not free
Laws dictate owners should agree
Not hearsay and jealous villagers
Who serve no useful purpose.

TU'IKETEI

He smiles like the Mona Lisa
Enjoys playing with his toys
And laughs at our funny faces
Now turning one blessed with rain

Life giving rain then sunshine
God's miracles on Waitangi Day
Taken for granted by men
Floating on a ball called earth

Creation of a Higher Being
That fill our lives with joy
One day he'll be a man
When I can no longer work

We take a walk on the beach
My cane holding me up
A fragile old man enjoying
The support of a grandson.

MY HOUSE

A plan for $1,000
To build my dreamhouse
For an $80,000 budget that failed
The architect planted tomatoes instead

My father build a shed on my land
To mark where I should be
When there is a hurricane
A refuge for ideas

A view like in heaven
Imagination of history
A port covered in ancient kalias
From faraway lands coming to trade

Mangoes fruit heavy each year
Logan species are sweet
A chestnut marks the road
With buses passing near

I dream of a roadside market
A bar with a view
When I retire and build it
A house and rooms to spare
Extension of past plans.

2. POEMS ABOUT LOVE AND DESIRE

MY LOVE

I saw you in my dreams
I saw you in your pictures
I saw you in your videos
And I feel I have loved you
All my life and a thousand years

Not because you have wealth
Or power and persuasion
A body of immeasurable beauty
But a loving heart that I can see
In your smile and eyes, I believe

But I know you are just an illusion
Not because you are a dream
Or floating flowers in a stream
I cannot touch and feel
You think that I am not real

Blessed is the salt that give taste to beef
Blessed are the spices making customers smile
Blessed are the people who love
For they shall be happy and gentle
Not growling lions when its time to eat

I am a fool in love
With your heart and smile
With your gentle touch and feeling
Come and take me with you
And make me yours for all eternity.

THE RIGHT REASON

Do things for the right reason
As sure as the four seasons
Do things the right way
Invite your angels to stay

The river runneth to the sea
As sure as rain cycles feed the trees
Oceans fly through the air
Clouds of hope not despair

Freedom is more than life
As precious as a loving wife
Millions have died defending it
Egypt, Babylon, United Nations, wit

Put your dreams on a rainbow
Drink happiness not sorrow
Fly to the moon like yesterday
I bid thy love on my heart to-day.

ONE DAY I SAW AN ANGEL

She was more beautiful
  Than my restless dreams
  Occupying my mind
  Like a helpless colony

Then I saw her twice
  Destroying my will totally
  I moved to sit under her
  Huge mango trees

Wishing she would fall
  From the cloudless sky
  And tell me it was mine
  Whatever the day or time

I sat under the mango trees
  Til they died of a fruitful old age
  And I sleep and sit there still
  In my unconscious mind

How unkind fate has been
  To rob me of that divine
  Revelation of the soul
  A beautiful shining damsel

I would travel there still
  Hoping to see that sight
  But my failing human-ness
  Knows it won't be thrice.

THE LOVING WOMAN

She brings out the best in her man
Cooks, cleans and kiss his hand
He worship the ground she walks
And love her all night till dawn

Roses grow fragrant in her garden
A beautiful sight each morning
He enjoys its heavenly fragrance
Her perfume as she clings to him

She noticed he is stronger
Pink, white and red petals
His body wrapped in aroma
As he worshiped her pedestal

Whispering in her ear
She whimpers and moans
Lovely endearing words to hear
As he climbs her throne.

Now it's time for him to leave
An overseas trip, a meeting
She cannot bear to be free
Of his presence, like a dream

Take me with you, she begs
Her hot breath on his chest
Caressing him with her legs
Just one more time in bed.

SMILE

I saw a twinkle in your eye
Is it for me or another guy?
Does your garden flower rain or sunshine
Will you come and be mine?

Smile and laugh it's the music
Love that does not miss a beat
Like flowers opening in a mist
Sparkling like diamonds and free

Do you dance for me or someone divine
A god or perhaps a handsome lad?
Lords of the earth design
A million reasons to be glad

Dance for me my angel
Dance for me my love
Precious moments, precious moments
Like my soaring dove.

LOVE

Feelings of a man for a woman
Sister, brother or a friend
A mother, father or relation
Forces driving reincarnation

Hunger for the flesh
Released from Hades
Desire to be satisfied
Caligula's fantasy fortified

A humming bird seeking honey
Babies crying for their mummy
Children clinging to their mothers
A man leaving one for another

No love is greater than he
Who said it was meant to be
To give his life for his friends
Divine love that never ends

Love means never be sorry
Be happy don't worry
She will always be there
Feelings, comradeship never wear

Charity for the unfortunate
A helping hand for your mate
Give your possessions to the poor
Then ask Jesus to open the door

Attraction is a beautiful thing
Affairs and swings
Crushes of immaturity
Loneliness in the city

Poetry in motion
Jealousies and commotions
Fishes in a school
Breaker of the rules.

SUNRISE

Her smile light up the sky
Rays of hope in the sunrise
Tuna feeding on a school of fry
Joyful and feeling divine

Shadows of gray
Disturb the glassy sea
Whisssh of waves
In Gulliver's world

Her tingling laughter
Disturb the birds
Fluttering on their perch
Crackling sounds on the sand

Tangaroa watched from the sky
Maui beckons her to his boat
Don't look at any other guy
All you need is my coat!

A BEAUTIFUL WOMAN

You love, cherish and worship her
She brings out the best in you
Warm your heart with joy everyday
She's loving and considerate
Lets you have your way

You care not for material things
A smile, a kind word, her cooking
You live only to look after her
The children and your dreams
No one else to interfere

Then one day she's gone
Your loving world collapses
Nothing matters anymore
Only the sound of tiny feet
Soothing your aching heart

Nothing is left but empty space
In your heart, head and place
Only the kids fill the vacuum
Vacant kitchen, bed and rooms
Where once lived a beautiful woman.

TWINKLING EYES*

I saw a twinkle in your eye
Is it for me or another guy?
Does your garden flower
Rain or sunshine?

Do you dance for me
Or someone divine?
A God or perhaps
A handsome lad?

Dance for me my angel
Dance for me my dove
Precious moments
Like my soaring love.

BEAUTIFUL ROSES*

Beautiful roses in your garden
I love to look on
Beautiful roses in your garden
I love to smell and touch

Beautiful eyes on your face
And sweet lips to kiss on
Beautiful roses in your garden
I love to lie on

Beautiful birds and bees
And honeydew in your kiss
Beautiful roses in your garden
I love to sleep on

Come away with me
Darling, come away with me
Come away with me
Darling, come away with me.

A GIRL IN TOWN*

There's a girl, in town
And she wants to know
If he love her, if he need her
For she may never come

There's a boy, in the village
And he wants to know
I she loves him, if she needs him
For he is in love

Her parents don't want him
Marry a boy in town
He is from the village
Poor, ragged, unhygienic

He stands at the altar
Waiting for her to turn up
But she changed her mind
One rainy night

He waited for her on the bed
She just smiled from the shadows
And disappeared into the dark
One rainy night

Take me to town, she said
A hotel room, motel or a club
Your bed and linen's too dirty
As she got into the taxi
One rainy night.

---

* - These poems are songs recorded on Youtube

A BOY IN TOWN*

There's a boy in town
And he wants to know
If she loves him, if she need him
She may not come to the wedding
She may not come to the wedding

There's a girl in town
And she want to know
If he love her, if he need her
He may not turn up at the wedding
He may not turn up at the wedding

He stood at the altar from morning til night
His guests so weary from standing up
She did not turn up at the wedding
She did not come to the wedding

One day he saw her dancing in a bar
Dancing in a bar til late at night
He walked in and looked at her
He could not believe his eyes

She smiled in the dark
A sad smile but delighted
I cannot sleep that night
I cannot sleep that night

My life is ruined, my life is ruined

See you at the motel
Don't look so worried
You don't need a piece of paper
To prove I am your wife.
She laughed, and she laughed.

AN ODE TO A PRINCESS

Her heart belong in heaven
Smiles like saints, eyes of Helen
A face to launch a thousand ships
In Troy she is the object of worship
A trace of a smile like the Mona Lisa
Beauty that drove Apollo to despair
She walks the land with grace
Lips of red, soft with embrace
Her satin dress against her face
Lover's hidden in time and space
Strong as the Gods of Olympus
Stylish like an Empress in Paris
He wish he knew how to win her heart
And take her home in his chariot of fire.

HEILALA

Yellow pollen cover the stigma
Fragrant air over the petals
Honey feeds ants and butterflies
Humming bees keep on trying

Colors of blue, indigo and green
Disguises by nature's screen
Harmony among the birds and bees
Invisible signals, evolutionary keys

Insects and bees run wild
From the fragrant tree
A woman dancing, like a fairy
Flowers dripping dew in January

A tree of ancient Polynesia
Mysterious, beautiful like Cleopatra
Garland of kings through the ages
Endowed wisdom like sages.

EYES

Beautiful lashes, blue iris
Angelic faces in Paris
Visions of color in Greenland
Thirty three reasons to be grand

Digital input like computers
A collection of gray matter
It's job is to show and serve
Mass of ganglia and nerves

Two shiny oceans on a globe
Directing bits to earlobes
Watery reservoir of the Pacific
General, conclusive, specific

Love emanating from a ceiling
Information on your feelings
Spread eagled on a dream
A flower popping on a stream.

YOUR SMILE

Come, I want to go
Meandering streams flow
Gracious body movements
Still photos capturing moments

A swaying green dress
Caressing your live flesh
Expressive hands tell a story
Of another era, full of glory

Protective tents and seawall
Ancient Gods hear your call
A lonely tree by the sea
Lovely dances for all to see

Traditions and kava ceremony
Drinks from a magic potion
A Spanish recipe from Columbus
Sweet dessert under the bush

The wind disturb her hair
Like dewdrops on roses there
Shiny, fresh and full of fragrance
Money rained from the audience

A maid put on her shoes
Such faithfulness, so true
She leaves to dance another day
The crowds are awed, they pray

Beauty is in the eye
Feelings take a bye
I'll put a ring on her finger
And take her to the altar.

JUST BECAUSE

I love you because you are like a goat
You provide milk to warm my throat
I love you because you are like a sheep
You provide wool to let me sleep

It's not because you follow me blindly
But you bleat with me nicely
Just don't roar like a lion
And drive me to zion

I prefer you to be a chicken
So you can wash my linen
And your beautiful eggs
Can also warm my legs

I once knew a fox
Who just loved my locks
But all she wanted to do
Was sleep under a tree

So my beautiful goat
Don't let me fall in the moat
Of your dreamy castle
But keep me in your cradle.

3. POEMS ABOUT WAR AND CONFLICT

VERSES TO A WAR

This ANZAC day I saw
How terrible it must be in a war
Millions of people still endure
Their memories so sure
Of their deaths
Lest we forget

The armed services did a parade
Each old soldier remembering his mate

Who died needlessly
Under the skies of Gallipoli
We say farewell
They died in a shell

The officials gave speeches
Of their landing on the beaches
Of Gallipoli in Turkey
Their bravery is the key
All their relatives cried
Over the way they died

We remember, we will remember
They were our members
Says the armed servicemen
And the reverend said, amen
To their prayers
Amen, said the mayor

Go now in peace
Now you have a lease
Of a better life
With your wife
Says the reverend
Lest we forget.

NEW ZEALAND AGAINST NUCLEAR SHIPS.

It was 1984
They made it into law
To ban all nuclear ships
From coming for a visit

David Lange and his advisors
Decided it was wiser
Just a coincident, George Orwell
Predicted the end of the world

Western countries were not impressed
New Zealand suffered from stress
The United States canceled all training
Army, Navy, Air Force as if it's raining

The Prime Minister went to Oxford
To debate his policy with the Lords
"Sir, let's debate at the stadium,
Your breath smells of uranium"

So they accepted it
The PM has some wit
Let's agree to disagree
Continue trading, training we'll see.

NINE ELEVEN

It was a weapon so vile
Using a jet plane as a missile
They said 3,000 perished
In the towers they cherished

They were symbols of wealth
Destroyed with stealth
The World Trade Centre
Osama bin Laden was the sender

It mobilized a nation
Every soldier to his station
They searched high and low
Keenly feeling the blow

Their spies said he is an Arab
Training terrorists with no cap
He may be in cahoots with Saddam
In the wilds of Afghanistan

The commander in chief gave the order
Let the air force cross the border
The planes came from near and far
To bomb Kandaha

They use smart bombs
Guided by computers
The soldiers shouted with glee
When they fly down the chimney

Then the spies said
He is in a cave with no bullets
Let's bring out the bombers
Use the cave buster

The bomber flew so high
Just a line in the sky
The bombs hit the ground
Erupted with a terrible sound

The waves killed everything
All around in a ring
Pierced the cave to the heart
To tear their flesh apart

Then the spies said he escaped
Went around the guards
So sure he is with Saddam
In town or a farm

They invaded Baghdad
Filled the terrorists with lead
The snipers can shoot a fly

From a mile with the scope on high

It was a fierce battle
Imperial guards got in the saddle
And run as fast as they could
The opportunists took the loot

Gold, silver, diamonds and cash
US dollars in Saddam's stash
They filled lots of trucks
Spoils of war, they made a buck

Then they found Saddam
Hiding underground, in a farm
People decided to hang him by the neck
With a rope until he is dead

They have conquered two countries
Grabbed everything like a breeze
But there is still no sign
Of the man they came to find

They say he has disappeared
His purpose as black as his beard
TVs plastered the world with pictures
In the Moslem world he is like Jesus

The war is over
Soldiers are bored
Just troublemakers and their crones
They can kill with their drones

The Pentagon got word
The Al Kaeta movement has spread
More terrorists are signing, said Al Gore
We hope it won't turn into a holy war

Let's kill the infidels
They shouted from their camels
President Obama had to go to Egypt
To calm them with his script

After 10 years of looking
It still came as shocking
They finally got it done
When they shot him in Pakistan.

They had to show some grace
And cannot expose his face
It was to be or not to be
So they buried him at sea.

WAR

There is no score in a war

You have to kill or be killed
They will steal your goods
And poison your food

There is nowhere to run
Everyone will have a gun
If you run for a while
They can shoot you from a mile

If they invade your town
They are evil not just clowns
Everything will be poisoned
Air, water, food, not just stolen

You will have nothing to eat
Eventually you'll lose your feet
There will be no water
They will rape your daughter

If you hide underground
Eventually you'll be found
But only the bones will be left
No one will know of your death

We all know they died needlessly
On the shores of Gallipoli
They can't return to their families
All that's left is their memory

It was a war to end all wars
In New Zealand 18,000 died
Fifty thousand were maimed
They cannot stand just lame

Then they started another one
Twelve million was the global count
Most of them were found
Generals and military men

When will they ever learn?
It's not like playing in a band
You have to kill
Or be killed.

MY ANCESTORS

Once we were kings
We were lords of the rings
They were allowed many wives
They were happy in their lives

The Europeans came
And joined in the game
They wooed the women
Who bore their children

They came from east and west
Have a woman if you pass the test
As long as the children stay
To look after the fray

It lasted fifty years
Of blood sweat and tears
But finally the youngest won
And turned the islands into one

After the battles
The King and chiefs settled
On a system
Imported from Britain.

THE MOSLEM WARS

Afghanistan fight the Taleban
Iraqis fight Iran and ISIS[1]
USA funds support armies
Of British, Israelis, Australians

Boko Haram steals girls
To sell to the highest bidder
Funding his guns and bullets
Rich Moslems the winners

Rebels run over the government
Demanding better governance
Jobs, business, education, health
And freedom in Yemen

Al Kaeta bombs America
With fuel filled planes
The World Trade Centre
Commerce and lives lost in the towers

Rebels shot down
Two Malaysian airline planes
Revenge for Moslem sins
Or unlawful plans

Jihadi John decapitates men
His family lives in London
Americans and Japanese lost their heads
Decorated apartments with flowers

The Syrian civil war
Displaced four million
Migrating to Lebanon
Germany and Britain

The USA want more
Australia and New Zealand
Save the Christians

From terrorist jihads

Desperate Mums, thousands of babies
Crying for their lost innocence
Outside the gates of freedom
Europe must find a solution.

---

1. Islamic State of Iraq and Syria

THE SAND DUNES OF HOPE

Eyes of the cold desert
  What are you fighting for?
  Hiding yourself from the air
  Your guns silent and cold

Lonely figures on the dunes
  Miles and miles of hope
  But nothing to show
  For 6,000 years of war

Abraham, Sarah, Hagar are gone
  So is Isaac, Ishmael and Jacob
  Only their names are still left
  In the troubled land of Israel

Eyes of the cold desert
  What are you calling for?
  I can see your shadows

On the vast golden waves

The wind is shifting the sand
   Spirits of war and angels
   Steel birds of prey' coming
   From far away lands

I can hear your war cries
   Violent, silent deaths inside
   The cavernous desert spirit
   What is it ,justice or revenge?

Do you melt into the night
   And join your ancestors
   Abraham's faith is right
   The ram's in the bushes.

THE STEEL BIRDS OF PREY

Small pockets of mushroom clouds
   Eight hits by the Russian jets
   Instant explosive destruction
   On the deserts of Syria

The rebels ran in fear
   Crying out to their Gods
   Baal stop the massacre
   Of our staunch rebels

We fight for freedom
  From the government
  We are not murderous terrorists
  Just disillusioned farmers

Cluster bombs like chain reactions
  Exploding dust balls into the air
  Thousands of years of travelers
  Through this ancient land

The new front in the ancient war
  That started between Ishmael
  And Isaac, fighting over a toy
  Steel birds of prey taking sides

Where Jesus struck Paul down
  For beating Christians and believers
  Where he was chosen by fire
  To spread the words of the gospel.

4. POEMS ABOUT EDUCATION

PURE RESEARCH

I make my observations
Like a divine revelation
I record the data
As often as I could muster

Then I form a hypothesis
To test for my thesis
Experiment, Experiment, Experiment
Prove the hypothesis by experiment

Then I form a theory
Accepted by the jury
Of my peers
With a few beers

Working in the lab is my way
Not sweating around in a plantation
I only like working in the lab
I hate doing field work

The Economic crisis
Forced the department to budget
Now my theory
Is becoming a target.

WHY AM I NOT RICH?

I was smart and good looking
Well mannered not shocking
Highly qualified and talented
I could leave most for dead
In a skill competition
But there ends my supposition

Like the philosophers say
It's just the world of to-day
They pay more for rugby players
And favor high flying lawyers
Because millionaires pay well
To get them out of jail
Eight hundred dollars per hour
Makes my $11 look sour
But I have a higher degree
I should not work for free
They said, sorry mate just get laid
As long as you are happy
And can afford a nappy!

MY PhD

I wanted to further my studies
Not to impress my buddies
Just a goal, not the dole
I just want to show
How far I can go
I think it's wise
Use micro-organisms like a vice
Which forces disease out
Just like a knockout bout
It will be safer for all
Than using chemicals
I could not find a supervisor

But none got wiser
You can still do it on a mission
With long distance supervision
It seems I am on a lurch
The trend is towards pure research
I thought it was a joke
You know he is the bloke
More intellectual content
It's worth millions in the future
It may not be useful now
But looking smart
Is better in a book!

AN ODE TO BEING SMARTER

Eating berries make me smarter
Improving my feelings matter
As long as I don't get fatter
Anti-oxidants and flavonoids
Not just good looking
It will improve my memory
I'll remember everything
The girls like smart boys
Even better than their toys
It just tickles their fancy
To come and talk to me
I am now interested in girls
I am coming out of my shell

Deodorants sprays and sweet smells.

UNIVERSITY DAYS.

I was so excited
As if I'm knighted
More than a pass
I needed in marks

It was a good year
But homesick as a bear
My relatives were kind
Education, improve my mind

In lectures I study cells
But only stared at a girl
Feeling like a sinner
Every time we had dinner

Eight science papers
As sharp as a saber
Drank too much beer
Enjoyed too much cheer

During exam time
I had plenty of time
Went to the pub
Had a little sup

My girlfriend went away
See you another day
She has decided it's time
To marry another guy

A job during the holidays
$158 was the weekly pay
It was enough for me
Saved heaps for next year

I went to Taupo
Drank enough for four
They have not seen
Underwater skiing

I told some tales
Just me and the boys
And a story for the rest
Of the penguins in the forest

I play rugby, billiard
Snooker, volleyball
Table tennis, wrestling
And teasing girls

In the first year
I was not too keen
But my advanced courses

Got only Bs and As

Then I did a Masters
Like looking for a new
Planet in space
Target was so small

Finding a virus
Under the electron
Microscope at high
Magnification

And developing
New antibodies
To a new virus
A test that works

I now realize
How hard it was
But I thought
Such excitement!.

. EDUCATION

My brain was empty
Then I learned the ABC
My mind was blind
Then I learned designs

Now I can see
As far as Eternity

I can work out
Why monkeys shout
The stars affect the mood
Like a puppy in the boot
It will cry, it's too shy
To ask and question why

I learned figures
Mixed with liquor
Hilarious results
Just the malts
In the whiskey
A watery key

Complex equations
Timetable in a station
Once learned, memorize
It will suffice
To guide you
All the way.

5. POEMS ABOUT ORGANISATIONS

THE UNITED NATIONS.

It has 191 members, a global government
Every country under the firmament
Signs its charter and testament
Established in 1945 during the war
USA, UK and USSR foresaw
The need for it to prevent wars

The decision of the Security Council
Is binding on all members
If they do not agree
They can sanction their supporters
And order ceasefires
Peacekeeping Forces intervene

The General Assembly
Controls most of its work
They work for free
Their countries pay their perks
They work tirelessly
Looking after its 6 branches

The Secretariat is controlled
By the Secretary General
He employs 25,000 professionals

From 160 Realms
They do not answer to their Governments
Only to the UN.

The International Court of Justice
Consist of 16 Judges
Appointed by the Council
To preside over their clashes
Of member States
Advise their Heads

The International Criminal Court
Has 18 Judges to date
Appointed by the States
To decide their politicians fate
If they decide to wage war
On their people with no law

The Economic and Social Council
Elected by the General Assembly
Supervises the work of the Committees
Commissions and Expert Bodies
In Economic and Social Areas
And Co-ordinates UN's Agencies.

SOUTH PACIFIC COMMISSION

It was established in 1947
By the Canberra Agreement
A product of World War II
By the Allies and their crew

It evolved into a technical organization
A mini United Nations
To carry out assistance for 22 Islands
With Australia, New Zealand, USA and France
The United Kingdom withdrew its support
It's responsibility is to its fort

The European Union is the new Britain
To support Africa, Pacific and Caribbean
A symbol of the new SPC[1]
From the Pentagon to the new edifice
On the beach of Anse Vata[2]
A memorial like no other

Its staff are all professionals
Who roam the Pacific and all the world
To bring knowledge and ideas home
To build member countries like their own
Fisheries, Agriculture, Women, Health
Every kind of intervention like a commonwealth

They took 8 years to decide
Whether the PPPO[3] is right
Legal assistance from FAO[4]
With diplomatic words just to show
If they want to join the IPPC[5]
The SPC Conference can do it for free

Then in 1996 they decided
To change the name they were delighted
With the new buildings
And the new wings
But forgot, I am missing from Camelot
Just as well, I am not a girl.

---

1. Secretariat for the Pacific Community is the new name for
the South Pacific Commission since 1996
2. Beach on the waterfront opposite the SPC headquarters in
Noumea, New Caledonia
3. Pacific Plant Protection Organization
4. Food and Agriculture Organization of the United Nations
5. International Plant Protection Commission

AN ODE TO THE USP

The University of the South Pacific
Was established in Fiji
By the leaders of the islands
To educate the Pacific's children
Even the men and the women

Thousands of the island's kids
Have developed their skills
Doctors, Lawyers, Teachers it's all they did
To promote learning, research and teaching
Infrastructure and job creation
A new ideal in respect and dignity
Logical application of philosophy
Education grows like a Christmas tree
Enlightenment that shines from USP.

THE COMMONWEALTH

They share all their money
And worldly belongings
53 countries, formerly colonies
The British build up their countries

Annual finance ministers meetings
Biannual heads meet
To decide all activities
In Education, Agriculture, Science

Countries come in
Others go out
Depends on misbehaving
And breaking the rules

Encouraging scholarship
In the young people
Scientists to create sheep
Producing more meat

Commonwealth students
Learn the history of Britain
Attend Oxford and Cambridge
Work harder and become rich

They leave their traditions behind
And adopt the Westminster Style
Constitutions and the rule of law
No more executions like before

Their countries grew in wealth
Better health, education and trade
Only dreams to create
With nothing to regret.

WELFARE DEPARTMENT

They keep people in dependency
For as long as they can cream
Everything from the system
Which can no longer assist them

Find a job that's your lot
You have lost the plot
Come to the seminar
And chat up the clerk

I attend the seminar everyday
There's no change to my pay
It's better with Enterprise Allowance
At least I can pay for my business plans

I have many products to sell
They are more interested in the bell
How about Parental Allowance?
I work as my children's accountant

Pay parents for their work
The dole people they are so slack
They never do anything
Except smoke dope and drinking

I wonder if they have a brain
They are working against the grain
You have to be serious
If you can't find a job start a business

Gareth Morgan and the millionaires
Proposed a universal basic income
To support small business and self-employed

Boosting buying power and billions created

But politicians are not too keen
All they need is to believe
It was not in their education
They have never been in business

If the farm paddock grass is stunted
Cows don't have enough to produce milk
Devastation for the dairy industry
New Zealand's largest export

Similarly, if 95% of business fails
Add some fertilizer to revive them
The word will spread creating growth
And help the people of New Zealand!.

6. POEMS ABOUT SPORTS

JONAH LOMU

He was a troubled kid
Who grew up on the street
Then he went to Wesley[1]
And learned to play rugby

It was said their first fifteen
Went through unbeaten

All the other schools
Got beaten by their mauls

He was only eighteen
When chosen by Laurie Mains[2]
The youngest ever All Black
To play in the backs

Every game made him famous
He always scores under the post
He was like a bulldozer
Plowing over tacklers

Then in the 1995 Rugby World Cup
The fans watched him in every pub
They slapped each others backs
When he ran over England's best

He scored four tries
And all the pubs ran out of fries
Everyone rejoiced in New Zealand
When the All Blacks beat England

Jonah became a superstar
They beat every team by far
It was all for one and one for all
When they got to the final

It was the All Blacks and the Springboks
They played like obsessed men
You could have heard a pin drop
When Jonah got the ball and ran

That was a sure try
We don't know why
The referee brought him back
The whole country went mad

They tackled everything that moved
But break some of the rules
So they got penalized
Bringing tears to the fans eyes

It was a game of penalty kicks
They have to throw in every trick
But both sides could not score
Every player tackled till he was sore

The referee extended the time
The score was 12 all
The All Blacks were in a line
When their first five dropped the ball

It flew and rolled towards the posts
Kiwis looked as if they saw a ghost
The ball went through the middle

And the referee blew his whistle

I have never seen All Blacks cry
But they were not shy
It was just the way they felt
In front of the world

Mandela[3] gave the cup to his captain
Who held it up like a lantern
As if to shine a light
To abolish apartheid

It was a fitting win
For Nelson and his team
I guess they got their inspiration
From his 27 years in prison

And the All Blacks went back
They had given their all
Jonah was just glad
He had answered their call.

---

1. Wesley College in Pukekohe just outside Auckland
2. All Blacks coach and selector
3. Nelson Mandela the President of the Republic of South Africa

RUGBY WORLD CUP 2011.

Richie McCaw [1]led out his team
They were all excited, they were keen
The final of the Rugby World Cup
Against the French at Eden Park
12 years in the planning
Have come to fruition
With the whole world watching

The All Blacks came through unscathed
Through the pools and earned their place
To play for rugby's most coveted trophy
The Web Ellis Cup from the town of Rugby
Where rugby started, where it all began
When a soccer player picked the ball and ran
And created New Zealand's most popular game

The fans from New Zealand and France
Are getting ready for the victory dance
The huge stadium was all quiet
When the first five kicked off
The forwards met with a mighty clash
Half back pass the ball to the backs
As the huge crowds chants

First five, second five to the wing
He passed the ball with a mighty swing

They stepped one, two, three, four
The gigantic crowd thought he will score
And erupted with a colossal roar
The French regrouped their defense
And forced the attackers to the fence

Now they stand for the line out
All Blacks, All Blacks, the fans shout
Kevin[2] threw the ball up to the lock
Who caught it in mid-air like a hungry croc
The forwards parted like the red sea
And Tony Woodcock[3] sailed through unseen
To score by the corner like a dream

It was 24 years in the making
Practicing this move while shaking
From the cold nights of winter
But it did not discourage or hinder
Their greatest wish, and ambition
To beat the opposition to submission
It's written on the wall, "Champions of the World"

The first five missed the kick
Each team build their attacks brick by brick
To and fro the teams played
As their fans grew more afraid
The French keep breaking the All Blacks line
Every time, they got stopped by a hair

And drove Colin Slade[4] to despair

Finally the French scored by the post
Their captain was gracious he did not boast
Now the score is lost to France 7 to 5
Which boosted the All Blacks with more drive
Piri Weepu[5] kept kicking and missing
And the crowd started shouting and hissing
Till Steven McDonald[6]kicked, they started singing
The All Blacks is finally winning
It was a war and battle not a game
It would have put the Spartans[6] to shame
The whole country beamed with pride
As Richie McCaw held the cup by his side.

---

1. All Blacks captain
2. Kevin Mealamu, All Blacks hooker
3. All Blacks prop
4. All Blacks first five
5. All Blacks half back
6. Replacement first five when Colin Slade got injured.

RUGBY WORLD CUP 2016

The All Blacks won the cup again
Through the rounds they were unbeaten
Just too strong, committed and believers
In their ability to be the winners

The first back to back win
The first team to win three times
Both records for captain McCaw[1]
Earning respect, a name for himself

New Zealand has proved too strong again
The All Blacks never looked weak in the rounds
Scoring higher than the opponents
In the mauls, rucks and broken play

But more devastating in formation
Daniel Carter[2], Ma'a Nonu[3,] Fekitoa[4]
To penetrate the defense like a plan
Going well from start to the end

I predicted a final with Australia
Two teams that stand out from the beginning
Wallabies is the team to beat, I said
And sure enough in the final

Israel Folau[5] was a devastating runner
But could not catch the wily Ma'a
Who dashed and stepped like a little boy
Going through his uncles and aunts

The Wallabies were not beaten, just smashed
Just what the Kiwi supporters wanted
To show the Aussies they have to come here

For a rugby scholarship and some beer

England was a gracious host
Showing, again, they are royal at heart
Staunch, one eyed supporters but not enough
To beat the best in the game.

---

1. Richie McCaw, All Black Captain
2. All Black first five
3. All Black second five
4. Malakai Fekitoa, All Black Center
5. Wallaby full back

CRICKET WORLD CUP 2015

Hit the ball as hard as you can
It's legal, you can beat it anytime
Run, run and run again
It's not a war, just a game
Many teams vie for the crown
Who's the best, the rest get out of town
We're it, don't argue with the champ
Just turn up at the celebration bbq

Clarke[1] claim Australia is the best
Vettori[2] bowled out the rest
And a spinning British press
Telling stories about phones
And beer taps

Then Chris Cairns got lbw
Fixing games and bending rules
From the ICC[3], Vincent and the captain
Squeaking in by a hair.

---

1. Australian captain
2. Daniel Vettori, Black Cap (NZ) spin bowler
3. International Cricket Council

THE OLYMPICS.

It was the sport of ancient Greece
As the promoter of the peace
Every warrior lay down his arms
To compete in the rounds

Javelin, jumping, athletics and discus
They competed on olympus
It is said they wore no clothes
To show off their muscle folds

Every lord worth his name
Must compete in the games
To display his speed and skills
As a battle of stamina and will

The winner gets a wreath
When he recovers his breath
Then wait for a hug and kiss

From the most beautiful miss

The games was abandoned
Competitors were not pardoned
By their mistress and missis
To compete in the games

After centuries in the dust
The French said its revival is a must
They started planning it
For the first game in 1896

It was a dream come true
Every country was given the rules
They will hold the Olympic games
Every four years with no change

The Olympic Committee
Oversees the bidding
Every city in the world
Want the Olympic Games

Then they build stadiums
Honor the winners on the podiums
The gold medalist at the Olympics
Outshine every other competition

More than 200 countries
Must put in their entries
Train for years in the rain and cold
In their dream of winning gold

The peak of all competition
A test of the human spirit
Beat the best in the world
Like winning your dream girl

It puts every country to elation
When they win the competition
Every parent feel so proud
When their child leads the race

The best of the human ideals
To showcase the way they feel
They forget all their shame
When they win at the Olympic Games.

THE HURRICANES

They call them the Hurricanes
In 1982 they won 14 of 16 games
They were all students and mates
In the Auckland first grade

They were unstoppable
Anyone can carry the ball
Their backs were all fast
With the first five leading the charge

A kick, a dummy then a pass
First the full back, center, winger last
He stepped one, two, three four
To the try line for a score

They call it second phase
Always give the opposition a taste
Of how fast they can regroup
Always scoring it was so good

The players have a lot of belief
So it was always a relief
That they can win every game
The supporters love their name

Then the other teams
Said there is no competition
They have to bend the rules
Changed our name to "Varsity Blues"

But it did not change anything
We may be a Blue but can sing
In the pub with some beers

We always win with some cheers.

SUPER FIFTEEN

It started in 1996
Just 12 teams to compete
Auckland was ruling the roost
Their fans consumed all the booze
Then the Crusaders took over
No more alcohol just Jehovah
They were winning every year
Deans was the Coach, it was clear
Then the Brumbies had a run
And got tackled just for fun
Gave the Sharks some more marks
It was the weekend routine
Watching the Super Fifteen
We used to make a lot of noise
Now I'm quiet, just the boys.

RUGBY LEAGUE

I was the standoff in our team
That was number six
My job was to pass the ball
And make sure my team is on a roll
I always position my kicks
When we reach tackle six

Straight into the corner
Up and under or a roller
Just to put one of my guys
With the ball over the line
Then I kick a goal
Straight between the poles
And jog back to my team with a grin.

SEVENS RUGBY

It lasts for seven minutes
But players need a lot of spirit
After three minutes of tackling
They will be ready for retiring

The Fijians were the masters
Of passing and throwing the ball
Between the legs, overhead and shoulders
They were winners overall

Then the Samoans had a run
And won some tournaments they had fun
They always know how to make the big hits
And pass the ball on their feet

England won the first World Cup
With their fans filling every pub
They certainly know how to celebrate

Their players know how to be great

But the New Zealand team
Knows how to win every time
They always score with stealth
Winning gold at the Commonwealth

Sevens rugby has brought enjoyment
To every major city where they play
Hong Kong, Wellington, LA, Dubai
The fans gulped their last beer with a sigh

Hopefully our team wins next time, they say
If not gold, the World Cup or just shine
So we'll buy some more beer
And create heaps of noise with our cheer.

THE AMERICA'S CUP 2013

Automated foils
Brilliant oils
Practical measures
Miracles and theory

An oracle or a message
For the future
UFO's[1] streaming through space
Flying boats, not a race

Upside down sails
Of the Polynesians
In San Francisco Bay
Double hulls of the millennium

A numbers game
Now in a name
Minus one to nine
In eleven wins, just divine

They say, we are obsessed
With the America's cup
You can have the rest
And a beer at the pub

Emirates can fly
But the Oracle[2] tells why
Technology is the miracle
Walk on water, wine for a tipple

Muscle, tactics and strategy
Supporters, money and teams
Of all the winning factors
Technology is the greatest.

---

1. Unidentified Flying Object
2. American yacht

7. POEMS ABOUT AGRICULTURE

THE FARMER

His grandfather was a share milker
Who bought a 2,000 hectare farm
Selling milk to Fonterra[1]
And make $400,000

Everything is going well
He also won his dream girl
Then the price of milk fell
And he has to cut and sell

Moving into town
Was the jewel in the crown
But all the diamonds fell off
They were worse off than Maddoff[2]

It was another Crafar[3] farm
With no hope of a rebound
Asking for a benefit was the last
Kick in the guts.

---

1. Fonterra – the largest dairy processor and exporter in New Zealand.
2. Maddoff – of the famous Ponzi scheme…and court case… in the American stock market…during the 2000s.

3. Crafar farm – was one of the fastest growing dairy farms in
New Zealand but was closed down with too much unpaid
debts, over $200 million.

THE TONGAN FARMER

He has eight acres of land
To grow crops for his family
Then sells the surplus
And plant a few trees

Mangoes, tava[1] and breadfruit
To supplement their food
The kids grew strong and tall
Helped with fishing and tourist stalls

He made $500 a day
When cruise ships visit
A clerks salary in a year
In the government offices

His fishing boats and net
Bring twenty strings a day
Sold at $3 each, that is $60 made
Pays his children fifty cents

Kids go to the movies
For ten cents entry
Five cents for roasted peanuts

Thirty five cents saved

I am rich, the farmer thought
The yam and crop harvests
Fit for a Christmas feast
Bring the whole family

All delicacies, roasted pigs and sweets
Piled high on the feast mat
Heavenly food for a kid
When the Reverend give thanks
For their plentiful harvests.

---

1 - Polynesian lychee or logan, *Pometia pinnata*

THE PLANTER

He plants yam, taro and cassava
Vegetables and maybe some kumara
Some pigs are in the pen
Chickens and a few hens

The family has a van
With plenty of root crops and melons
And some to barter and sell
In the village he is doing well

The Tongan Rugby Committee
Selected him to the National Team
They toured Australia and Fiji
New Zealand and Britain

He scored one try
But their team got fried
By all the other teams
They lost by 150 points but tried.

THE WATERMELON PLOT

Mark the rows on prepared land
Each mound and soften the soil
Mixed with 200 grams fertilizer
Plant the seeds two weeks later

Watch the growing seedlings
For aphids, slugs and disease
Apply chemicals if required
Mulching under the creeping vines

Cover the second fertilizer application
Under plenty of top soil
Just under the emerging flowers
And young shiny melons

Spray for insects and disease
Every two weeks
Keep the vines healthy
With producing fruit

Keep weeds at bay
With vines free
As more melons emerge
Fill the water tank

Spray the melons
With the mist blower
Water from the tank
Chemicals from town

On rainy drizzly days
Behold the sight from your house
The hundreds of whitish melons
Among the green leafy ground.

WASHED AWAY

They rarely flower these days
Thousands of mango trees
Just mountains of dead leaves
To show for their existence

Necrotic spots on the young leaves
A symptom of the disease
Waiting to destroy flowers
As they emerge each season

The villagers pray for a miracle
When millions of flowers emerge
They hope for sun not rain
Which wash away the emerging fruit

Scientists sprayed the trees
With chemicals from overseas
Benlate[1] mixed with manzate[2]
To control anthracnose[3]

The mangoes were saved
Heavy branches bend from fruits
Fruit bats grew fat and breed
A thousand more seedlings grew.

---

1. A systemic fungicide (work inside the plant)
2. A contact fungicide (work on the surface of the plant)
3. A fungal disease caused by the fungus *Colletotrichum gloeosporioides* which attack a lot of crops.

THE TOMATO FARMER

On Sundays he preach for Christ
After hard work on Saturdays

Sowing the seedbed and posts
For the early tomato season

Seedlings come up for light
Getting ready to transplant
Moneymaker grow fast
Heavy with fruit and leaves

When they were mature and ripe
He invite church goers to come
Harvest the bountiful fruits
Wheelbarrows were filled

They worked from dawn til dusk
Five hundred cartons were packed
For Turners and Growers in Auckland
From the tomato farmer of Pukekohe

They celebrate with a feast
His first load sold on the day
At fifteen dollars a carton
He feels like a rich man.

A VEGETABLE GARDEN

Seeds carry genes for a million years
A present from the Gods in a packaged seal
Carrots, beans, parsley and melons

For the kid to water every day

He delights in his work
Nursery learning management
Excited by little tiny plants
Appearing where seeds were sowed

They grew big with luxuriant growth
Looking forward to the harvests
Pok choy and carrots are favorites
And mouth watering melons

Taro plants grew leaves so big
They obscure the lawnmower
Sunday recipes in coconut cream
Meat lovers tasting like a dream.

THE ROCKMELON

A yellow   aromatic ball
So inviting on the supermarket shelf
Bought by a rock melon fan
For the price of an apple
Covered in cling plastic
With yellow flesh inviting

A bunch of seeds
Buried in fertile ground

Grew where commercial seeds failed
Transplanted across the garden
To produce fruit from every shoot

Fertilizer boost the growth
Generate more fruits for the kids
Who love to eat melons
And good for their health

They look like Granny Smith apples
No bigger than a large marble
But sure to grow faster to many times the size
Looking like a taro ripened on the shelf.

8. POEMS ABOUT PLACES

OUR STREET

They say only marijuana dealers
Live on our street
Everyone else is a squealer
Avoiding the beat

Dirty little kids
Run around the kerb
Parents go to meet
The reverend in church

Rich girls and boys
Come in flash cars
Asking for dope like toys
They won't go far

We say, strawberries are in the shops
Grass grow on the lawn
Just ask the cops
If you need a joint.

ROME

Classy ancient hotels and delicious food
Then a visit to the catacombs
To view   early Christian tombs
Under the ground of Rome

The Parthenon and water canals
Cobble stone streets, ancient chariot tracks
To-day's soup in a special cafe
A bottle of wine and pizza til late

Crowded streets of the Colosseum
Tourists taking pictures
A monument to past emperors
Armies exterminating Christians

Past Popes line the Vatican cemetery

Under St Peter's basilica dome
Headquarters of Christianity
Where Roman soldiers used to rule

Op-shops filled with souvenirs
Of the cross, Christ and the Vatican
For all the tourist and local trade
Papal blessings take pride of place

A visit to Naples and Pompeii
Buried by Mt Vesuvius in 70 AD
Fossilized humans and babies
With silent screams on their faces

Then it's time to come home
After meetings and discussions
Global Plant Quarantine Standards
FAO, WTO[1], United Nations.

---

1. World Trade Organization

THE HUT

I am not happy in an empty
Glittering house full of
Valuables and silence
But my little hut that reminds
Me of the windy place

Where King Arthur and dragons lived
A forest of leucaena and guinea grass
Wild cocks with calls of solitude
Looking for a mate among the taro
So big they look like trees

Huge watermelons covered in dew
Hundreds lying on our field
An awesome sight for a child
Who loves the juicy fruit
At the new year banquet.

THE PALACE

It was called Tu'i Malila
Meaning he is a dwarf king
A present from Captain James Cook
Two hundred years before
Maybe he knew I would see it

Then I heard it died in a fire
A playful creature like a dog
Hiding its head under its shell
When I put my foot too close
A single tortoise in the Kingdom

The palace always look empty
No insects, birds or noise

Just silent forlorn trees on grass
Looking like expensive imported carpets
Only the statue like guard standing there

The crashing waves on the reef beyond
Sounds of spirits from Pulotu[1]
Dancing under the seabed
To the beat of Maui's[2] drums
As if to waken that ancient, silent house'

---

1. – Land of the Spirits in Tongan mythology
2. – One of the Polynesian Gods

MU'A

I go there every school holiday
A magical ancient village where Kings ruled
When giant Kalias[1] sailed the Pacific oceans
Now overgrown langis[2] with forgotten landscapes

Mary Lawry[3] wrote the beach was sandy
With water so clear you can see the bottom
Covered in mangroves and muddy runoff
The price of agriculture development

The aroma of roast pigs filled the air
Evoke a beautiful Christmas feeling
Fat sizzling on hot ambers

The 'umu[4] filled with delicacies

Mandarins and oranges are in season
Branches bending with fruit
All gone with the wind
Destruction of a virus

Fishing and swimming all day
A catch worth a month's wages
And payment of movies and peanuts
The balance to buy some bread.

---

1. Large ancient canoes
2. Ancient burial pyramids of Tongan Kings
3. Wife of Rev Walter Lawry, a missionary to Mu'a, Tongatapu, Tonga Islands in 1822.
4. Polynesian earth or underground oven

9. POEMS ABOUT NATURAL DISASTERS

CHRISTCHURCH EARTHQUAKE!

The Christchurch earthquake
Shook us awake
Of nature's terrible power
After quakes like a shower

The houses crumbled
The buildings crumbled

Skyscrapers fell
Like stones into a well

Dust flew
Everyone turned blue
They lost so much
Into the dust

We will rebuild it
Reinforce it
Was the plan
Of the land

They counted the cost
All seems to be lost
Too many people died
Billions of dollars lost

We should have foreseen
What should have been
Done to our city
Oh! What a pity!

Then money flowed
A waterfall into a city
The Mayor and the people smiled
Easy as running a mile

The Government regrouped
Neighboring Islands sent soup
Tonga sent watermelons for 1000
The Mayor said it should be 300,000!.

10. POEMS ABOUT RELIGION

POSSESSIONS

Casino tower beckons
Neon lights and barons
Pokie machine tunes
To pass the days in June

Mt Eden sights by day
Beauty and riches sway
City of endless lights
Decisions to stay and fight

Build a better future
Close the wound by suture
Caused by urban destitution
Products of civilized substitution

Life is not made of possessions
Said the father during confession
Strive for something that matters
Follow Jesus to the letter.

CREATION

In the beginning there was God
Weaving spells of magic words
Let there be land and seas
Air, animals and trees

Then he saw it was good
Animals, fishes and food
But something is missing
Man to rule with reason
He was created from the dust
His destiny to be just

Adam was his name
Lord of the Garden of Eden
God saw he was lonely
And created Eve to keep him company
A rib from his side
His own flesh to create his wife

They lived happily in peace
The serpent was jealous like a beast
Is it true you cannot eat, he ask
The forbidden fruit ?
You will become Gods, he says
And learn his clever ways

Eve was tempted and she took
A bite from the fruit
Of good and evil
Her eyes were opened
She realize she is naked
And her life full of problems

Adam out of love for his wife
Sacrificed his life
By eating it too
The serpent had them fooled
They ran and hid in the trees
But nothing can cover their grief

Did I not forbid you
From eating that fruit?
You will be punished from Eden
Eat bread from the sweat of your brow
Bear children in pain
They shall never enter the garden

Serpent, you will crawl the earth
And eat dust till death
God's punishment for every snake
Troubles for his jealousy
Harvests of his trickery
The betrayer of Eve

Adam and Eve left the Garden
And wandered the earth
They bore 2 children
Cain and Abel
One was a grower
The other a herder

They decided to offer sacrifices
Of animals and spices
To please God
But who would have thought
That Cain would offer his worst?
And Abel his best?

God saw evil in Cain's heart
His did not accept his plants
But looked on Abel with favor
His best meats to savor
A hard working lad
Who made his parents glad

Cain was as jealous as the serpent
And murdered Abel with his hands
God punished him to wander
The earth forever
And put a mark on his forehead
As a warning to the living and the dead

Adam and Eve bore another child
Seth was a lot more mild
And many more children
From God in Heaven
Such is the story of creation
Man became many nations

His descendants will be like sand
Or the stars of the heavens
Inhabit all the lands
Grew with their relations
At the end there's God
Weaving magic with his words

THROW THE FIRST STONE

There was a widow
Who was just a minnow
Then she met a man
To till and farm her land
But the neighbors were jealous
Of her wealth and success
Accusing her of adultery
To be stoned till death
The Lord said to them
What is your problem?
Let he who has no sin
Cast the first stone

They were all ashamed
With only themselves to blame.

JESUS

He stands at the door
And plead forever more
Let me dine with thee
Give your heart and mind to me
I will take your sins away
And the holy spirit will stay
To cleanse your soul everyday

Let me show you the power
Of faith and our belief in God
He is now and the future
Love and honor the Lord
Everyday and forever
Like the universe
He still expands

Millions of galaxies
Exist because you believe
What you see
Like the birds and the trees
But does your mind
Can see the designs
The hand of the creator

He speaks to you everyday
Come here, don't go that way
He whispers to the wind
To take away your sins
A burden of wicked men
It is written in the stars
What's in their heart

The universe is revealed
To men who believe
Their minds cannot deal
With the vastness of it
They still act like little boys
And thinks it's a toy

One day man will realize
That they have God in their lives
All they have to do
Is believe in his rules
First invite him in
To take away their sins
Then he'll do his part
In changing their hearts.

THE DEVIL

The bible say, he is Lucifer
An angel of the stars

He was next only to God
But he thought he is the Lord
He disobeyed and vanished
And was forever banished
To become the evil one

He wanders the earth
And claim everyone since birth
He corrupts them with his evil ways
Till the end of their days
Then God became a man
To help them understand
When their earthly body die
They can have everlasting life

His death and resurrection
Is the key to their salvation
When dust returns to dust
He will claim their spirit, God is just
And the evil one will have to run
When God takes over
He will have no fun.

THE HOLY SPIRIT *

Welcome Jesus
Welcome Jesus
Into my heart

Into my heart
And wash my sins away

The Holy Spirit
Is his promise
Which has saved
And healed the world

I've been saved
And I live
To make my way
Into heaven

Whoever believes
His reward is eternal life
Singing praises of God
Singing praises of the Lord

Just say the word Lord
And you'll save
The poor people of the world
Just say the word Lord
And you'll save
The sinful people of the world.

---

* - This poem is also a song I recorded and uploaded to
Youtube.

THE POOR WOMAN

I don't stand in street corners
  To proclaim my faith for all
  I don't go to church everyday
  I know, Jesus lives within me

Don't be like the Pharisees
  And criticize the faithful
  Or teachers of the law
  And crucify the disciples

Be like the poor woman
  Who had nothing left
  But a coin in her purse
  She gave the lord her all

Don't be like the ministers
  Who sit at the front and smile
  Feeling important and wise
  Be like a child of the kingdom

The kingdom of heaven
  Is only for the faithful
  Not the rich or important
  When you die, only faith lives.

MAN'S DESTINY

Man was born sick with Adam's sin
Cancer, dementia, asthma, disobedience
To the rules of Eden and God's plans
Only Eve did not understand

Man started dying when he was born
Only God's grace made him what he is
When he was saved by Christ
On the cross and the resurrection

Death was part of his being
When Lucifer fell from the heavens
Kept hidden til he is ready
Who can say no when God calls?

Don't be surprised no one lives forever
Just specks of dust returning to earth
Only the Higher Beings return to God
Cleansed of their sins, the destiny of man.

ISHMAEL

They believe in Allah
  God of their ancestors
  The promised land
  Moses, Jesus and Judah

Descendants of Ishmael
  Left the promised land
  To wander the desert
  Now they make a claim

Brother Isaac got the blessings
  The land of milk and honey
  Ishmael and his mother
  Became wanderers forever

Islamic Iraq and Syria
  They carved their State
  Made of guns and bullets
  Sharia laws and death

Now fighting the world
  Every country and religion
  War additions to their woes
  Wishing Hagar bring a solution

Oldest son of Abraham
  Now the sacrificial lamb
  On the altar of freedom
  For the rest of the world.

11. POEMS ABOUT PERSONAL PROBLEMS

GOVERNMENT INTERVENTION.

I am a writer
But just a pauper
Government's money
For the dope smokers

They prefer to drink beer
And have a bit of cheer
They are all depressed
Suffering from too much stress

I am a parent
Looking after children
I get nothing from anyone
No dollars to look after my son

Government officials give speeches
We are all unemployed
What about the UBI?[1]
To turn our children into something

They turn out to be lost
Stealing food to lessen the cost
And what the Government cannot give
Looking to other kids for a repeat

The crime rate has gone up
They spent all the money in the pub
Then got drunk and crashed

On the road instead of bed

The Government legal aid
Save the criminals, they said
Instead they put more funds
To house him, guard him with a gun

The PM laments
Our state is under mend
There is too much crime
Our children die in their prime

No one knows why
He is just another guy
But they continue to give money
To the dope smokers and their honey.

---

1. Universal Basic Income proposed by Kiwi millionaire Gareth Morgan and others.

DIVORCE

Wife take your boyfriend
  And go see the world
  Me and the kids will stay
  The grandchildren as well

Me and the kids plan
  To have a home garden
  Of melons, corn, silver beet
  The grand-kids can weed

I want to teach them
  To be self sufficient
  Smart and innovative
  To use their brains

Wife when you come back
  You can take the boyfriend
  And see the kids, grand-children
  Tell them where you been

I am sure they will be impressed
  With all your money and travels
  Then take off again to other lands
  Where you can adopt some animals

We prefer it together here
  I like gardening and beer
  Not sharing underwear
  Swearwords and stares.

12. POEMS ABOUT PEOPLE

OKINAWA

They have more old people
It's true not just a giggle
They always have some sake
With their parte

Sake is good
It puts you in the mood
For a tipple
And a giggle

That's why they live longer
Their hearts are stronger
It's a dream in Japan
Just like Peter Pan

Even the Police
With all their cheese
Cannot stop their hearts
With a letter from the judge

Now the old people of Okinawa
Can even climb a tower
Their legs are so strong
Drinking can't be wrong.

THE ENGLISH GENTLEMAN

I heard of him since I was little

He likes to have a tipple
Then have a posh dinner
Always feeling like a winner

He saves his money
For his honey
And a trust account haven
For his children

A castle is his fort
He likes to be the lord
Charity is his motto
If he's lucky and wins the lotto

Then he will buy a bike
And goes for a ride
He got hit by a trike
And got up and apologized.

13. POEMS ABOUT EMPLOYMENT

MY JOB

I am forming a hypothesis
To test for my thesis
I record the data
For my computer
I analyze the results

For my pals
Who will criticize
The size
Of
My
Figures with their reasons
Might as well look
In my book
And my conclusions
It's not an illusion
The maths speak for the paths
Of the unseen bugs
That spread the virus
Causing the disease
In our crop
As if
You
Robbed
The growers of their powers
To make some cash
For their stash
To help their wives
Improve
Their lives
And
The children
And their women
Now he is getting old

He
Walks with a stick
He march with a click
He has a lot of cash
In his stash.

CO-ORDINATOR

My contract with the South Pacific Commission
Says I will do everything without omission
27 member countries
Trust my decisions
Millions of dollars at my disposal
And I can write more proposals

Plant Protection Service
That is our greatest success
The Biosecurity of 22 Pacific entities
Solutions against weeds, insects, plant disease
Members of the Pacific Plant Protection
Organization
Under the auspices of the United Nations

The International Plant Protection Commission
Prepares documents for our revision
Experts in phytosanitary measures
Food and Agriculture is our treasures
Regional Plant Protection Organizations

Meet in Rome for more submissions

Fruit fly, taro beetle, biological control
Plant Protection in Micronesia and overall
In every mountainous island and atoll
Tissue Culture for hurricane recovery
Equipment, training, information in every territory
To improve the income, food security for every
family

The CAB International
Came with a proposal
To identify our flora and fauna
Every micro-organism in our corner
Pacific Biosystematics Network
Is a name to respect

Sixteen million American dollars in projects
Put more money in Pacific Islanders pockets
Biosecurity, Food Security and training
More dollars in Island Government savings
No holds on the expenditure
To build them a better future.

EMPLOY YOURSELF

Some people say they are unemployed
It means there's nothing to fill the void

Left by his former Boss who did it
Inspiration, motivation, self-belief and wit
Prove to others you are not stupid

Produce your own goods and services
Lawn mowing, sales, clean the terraces
Write, fight, trade-me and the races
Delivery, cook, door knocking, fishing
Co-operatives, imports, singing

There's a million things to be done
Work for yourself if not for someone
Knockers will always criticize
You know they are really unwise
They are negative about everything

Fight to protect yourself
Argue and reason with every person
Plan to win and succeed
With your every business
It is very simple just believe.

PANELA RESTAURANT

Hawaiian pizza steaming with aroma
Unforgettable cheese and pineapple
Sprinkled with sliced mushroom
A recipe for a special occasion

Lasagnia is on the menu
With garlic bread and red wine
A Mediterranean delight
Ravioli, potatoes and celery

I eat olives by the dozen
Every night while making salads
Ham wrapped in crisp lettuce
Cheese and heavenly dressing

Cassatta and Irish coffee
To complete my meal
Finished off with some brandy
Before I ride my wheels

A white twelve speed bike
As swift as the morning breeze
Across the Auckland domain
Heading home for some sleep

Dissecting dogfish the next day
Is not my idea of a complement
I'd rather be sitting in the park
Watching seagulls with my girl.

14. POEMS ABOUT FOOD

SALT

What is the most valuable
Commodity in the world?
Is it gold, silver or a girl?
Dreams to fulfill or dwell?

Serve me silver or gold
With my hot steak
It's too hard and cold
My teeth will break

Serve me a girl with my mash
My steak does not taste
Or a million dollar stash
Until you add sodium chloride

Salt, the most ancient trade
The ocean will not feel right
Next only to a beautiful baby
If you remove salt from the tides.

KIWI FOOD

I bought some kumara
To eat with my snapper
Coconut cream and mussels
A few bottles of bubbles

A leg of lamb on Sunday
Mashed potato and satay
A salmon from the stream
And some kiwi-ice cream

We can have some pavlova
Chuck everything in the rover
A picnic on the beach
Barbecue and some peach

Every kind of sausage
To go with fresh bread
And numerous brands of butter
Sunrise, country-soft spreader

Then we'll have some fruit
They all taste so good
Apples, pears and grapes
In all kinds of shapes

I can have some wine
If you'd be so kind
A chardonnay, merlot, chiraz
In a tinkling sparkling glass

I like cocktail tomatoes
Goes well with nachos
With all kinds of meat

I enjoy and love to eat

My daughter likes marmite
With her toast and fries
They say it will be back
For less than five bucks

Berries will make you smart
With marmalade jam in a tart
It won't put your brain in a twist
No need for a psychologist

Kiwifruit is making a billion
Mussels and salmon 700 million
Oysters, cockles and paua[1]
Fritters and fish in flour

There is plenty of food to mention
Vegetables, fruits and raisins
And legumes and beans
All good for your genes.

---

1. A Maori name for a shellfish

TASTEBUD HEAVEN

Nibbles with clipped ends
Heat the pot and olive oil

Add crushed garlic to the pan
Wait for fragrance to rise
Throw in a chopped onion
Ginger and your opinion
Then chicken already chopped
Garam masala, turmeric, stir
A little ginger to taste
More spices if you like
Cover on low heat
Til it's ready for the kids
A dish fit for a King
And friends to eat
Like a dream.

15. POEMS ABOUT THE ENVIRONMENT

GLOBAL WARMING.

Lightning breathed life
Into inanimate compounds
Cells with no wife
Doing the rounds

Amoebas[1] swim
In the primordial soup
And evolve into animals
Dancing in a loop

They grew eyes and fins
Mouths and swim
In search of food
It was plentifully good

Then they grew legs
And climbed into the land
Gave rise to a monkey
The ancestor of man

The air was so clean
Their noses had no sieve
Diseases were rare
No pollution there

The monkeys became smart
And developed tools
Air pollution were just farts
And odor from their stools

They became more industrious
And more handsome
Converting raw materials to pass
Inviting foreign workers to come

They build cities
Vehicles and trains
Drilled for oil and titties[2]

And fly in aeroplanes

Trees grew like weeds
From the plentiful carbon
And shed all their leaves
From acid rain and warmth

The warm seas
Are killing the food chain
Scientists research the pieces
Concluding its thawing ice, not rain

Sea level rise
Islands go under
Don't act surprised
If it drowns Kiribati

Fogs are common
In all large towns
Environmentalists say its smog
From all the burning grounds

Cancers are rising
From all the pollution
Be wise like King Solomon[3]
And create a solution

Many civilizations
Have gone before
And drowned in their pollution
Chemicals, CO_2[4], not just rotting floors

Many organizations
Try to reverse the trend
SPREP[5] and the United Nations
And in many other lands

There is still time
To clean up the earth
Or we'll stand in line
To farewell the dead

And return to the primordial soup[6]
From whence we came
Amoebas dancing in a loop
With no one to blame.

---

1. Amoeba – a single celled animal that move by changing its shape
2. Titties – Female breasts. A humorous reference to the popularity of sex as humans evolve.
3. King Solomon – a wise king according to bible stories
4. CO2 – carbon dioxide
5. SPREP – South Pacific Regional Environmental Programme
6. Primordial soup – refers to the surface of the earth in the early days…before animals evolved… when the

atmosphere was "toxic methane" and the surface was
like "mud" known as the "primordial soup".

THE OXYGEN CYCLE

God said
Let there be life
And it was done
Adam[1] needs a wife
He was the only one

God took his rib bone
And created her
But she was mostly stoned
From the marijuana air
She ate the forbidden fruit
And drove Adam to despair

They were banished from Eden[2]
To wander the barren Earth
They learned to reproduce
And Eve[3] gave birth
To Cain[4] and Abel[5]
Boys not angels

Their descendants
And all their animals
Breathed life to plants

The oxygen cycle
To keep them alive
Air from the primordial soup
Plants turning carbon into food.

---

1. Adam – the first man according to the bible
2. Eden – the Garden of Eden in the book of Genesis in the bible
3. Eve – the first woman according to the bible
4. Cain – the first son of Adam and Eve
5. Abel – the second son of Adam and Eve

THE FOOD CHAIN

Whales are so large
They break all scales
Eats plankton and fast
To reproduce in winter

Fish eats plankton too
And provide food
For animals bigger than them
Energy channels, not a problem

The sun gives energy to plants
And the plankton
Waste chemicals from land
Accumulate in animals

Man sits at the top
Accumulating poisons is his lot
From all the plants and animals
In the food chain.

ACID   RAIN

It's like bald patches
In pictures from space
Dead trees like rashes
On a baby's face

Factories and vehicle smoke
React with clouds up top
To lower the pH[1]
Creating acid rain on crops

It kills trees
Not just defoliating leaves
Destroys fishing fleets
From the empty seas

Dead rivers flow
Like the poisonous blood
Old men look like crows
Carcasses from Noah's[2] flood

---

1. pH – the concentration of ions in a liquid showing whether it is basic (pH that is higher than 7) or acidic (lower than 7).
2. Noah – "Noah and the flood", one of the famous stories from the bible.

OUR ISLANDS

Tuvalu is under water
Bubbling from the ground
Like lambs to the slaughter
There is no future

It's the rising sea
They showed on TV
Just one foot of water
Covering the floors

The land is sinking
Turn the rubbish into bricks
Show the world you are thinking
To save your beautiful islands

Neighboring islands are no better
They cannot be saved by a letter
The world has to do more
Reducing greenhouse gases like before.

GREENHOUSE GASES

Earth is like an egg yolk
Surrounded by the white atmosphere
Keeping all waste gases in bulk
Trapping the sun's rays in the air

Forests are carbon sinks
Absorbing accumulating gases
Like having a bubbly drink
Assets for investors to purchase

Plant trees in the desert
To open your carbon account
Create paradise in places
With no trees to count

The rising temperature
May become normal
Reductions in expenditure
And regrowth of coral.

ENERGY

The Big Bang[1] created
An expanding universe
Collapsing energy in places
Forming stars and planets

Nuclear fusion created the sun
Life giving energy to plants
Creating protein and carbohydrates
To feed the whole planet

Energy is passed on
To feeders and predators
Building bone, muscles, and neurons
Growing bigger than before

Some energy escape as heat
To warm their bodies
Their life cycle is complete
Nutrients for worms to eat

Plant roots absorb nutrients again
To create more food
And fulfill all of God's plans
Nature is so good

Only 5 billion^2 years left
Of life giving energy from the sun
Then it will expand before death
And consume everyone

Earth will be no more
Energy return to space
We cannot destroy it

Nor create[3.]

---

1. The Big Bang Theory – the most famous theory about the origin of the universe
2. 5 billion years left – according to scientific theory, the sun is halfway through its cycle of 10 billion years before it runs out of fuel.
3. Energy cannot be created or destroyed – scientific laws propose that energy cannot be created or destroyed, only transformed from one form into another.

THE POLLUTED RIVER

Rivers run clear
With overhanging plants
Filled with fish and deer
Protein for everyone

Then they build a factory
To process the sheep and cattle
Powered by coal from ancient trees
Filling the air with soot like a kettle

Animals release methane into the air
Their ammonia filled urine runoff
The river turns muddy and share
Stinking waste and fishes cough

New species arose
Others disappear
Artificial selection like prose
Evolution filled with tears.

DRIFTWOOD

The island people collect from their shores
Wood keep fires burning 'umu like before
A present from Maui and the Gods
Feeding people and their children

After 200 years of development
There's no more wood just plastic
Bottles, bags, floating nets under the pier
No more gods, fire or magic

Birds drop from the sky
Fish float in the seas
They ask the doctors why
Poisoned and cannot see

Seas bubble up the cracks
Of the sandy ground
Export of fish to overseas markets
None can be found

Crops fail each year
Now they eat rice
Imported from Indonesia
At a cheaper price

They have to leave their island
And live in another country
The environment's poisoned
Now they work, nothing is free

And the old people remembered
The ancient stories of old
Maui and their sky gods
Which made their people bold

It is all they have left
Stories of their island history
Driftwood to fill their plates
Eating under a tree.

MANGROVES

Their roots breathe
And hold silt there
Or the land will waste away
From the seas, waves and spray

Fish feed under their leaves
And sleep under trunks
Spawn between the roots
Providing predators with food

Coastal people use the wood
To build homes, pens and fires
Trap craps, sell more goods
To traders and labor for hire

Plant mangroves around the island
Its roots are strong to bind
Your land and sand together
Once grown, hurricanes will not matter.

THE OZONE HOLE

Scientists have proved
We need the ozone layer
To keep out ultraviolet rays
Which may cause cancer

But it's being depleted
By CFC[1] and other gases
From spray cans and fridges
We don't want burning faces

$O_3{}^2$ is the formula
Just oxygen with one extra
They have a worldwide ban
Change the gases in fridges and cans

The ozone hole closed again
And gave hope to the future of man
We will last a few years longer
With protection from the ozone layer.

---

1. CFC – clorofluorocarbon
2. O_3 – the formula for ozone

THE POLES

The North and South Poles
Are so wild and cold
Rain will freeze in the air
Much of earth's water are collected there

The arctic and antarctic ice area
Are bigger than Australia
If all the ice and snow melt
It will drown many islands in the world

A few degrees rise in temperature
Is all the ice and snow need
Increase all expenditure

Prevent accumulating carbon

A dog pants to cool itself
The atmosphere lets out heat
To cool the whole world
Or islands drown with nothing to eat

Our environment is very frail
Unseen dangers with no trails
It's good we understand
Keep nature in balance is the plan.

THE DEAD REEF

They say it was a hurricane
That killed the reef
But there was none in our area
Perhaps its agricultural urea

Scientists tested the water
No poisons were found
Just increases in temperature
Silent killers with no sound

The sun, giver of energy and life
Provide nice tans for your wife
Is the source of the heat
The ozone hole we cannot beat

Accumulating carbon
From all the pollution
Traps the heat in the atmosphere
A recipe for disaster

Everything is safe
When nature is balanced
Man is in strife
From his own activities.

DEFORESTATION

The Amazon[1] forest
Helps clean the air
By absorbing carbon dioxide
Greenhouse gases too

CO^2 is turned into oxygen
Carbohydrates and water
Cooling the air like a fan
Air conditioned fodder

Then commercial logging
Clears vast areas
With slow replanting
Carbon account arrears

In Papua New Guinea and Asia
Africa, Solomon Islands and Indonesia
Logging moves at a fast rate
With new trees to replace.

---

1. The Amazon river and surrounding forest in Brazil is one of the biggest 'carbon sinks' on earth.

16. POEMS ABOUT LEGENDS

KUPE'S SONG

Aotearoa[1], the long white cloud
Not a single bird in sight
As Kupe[2] bit into his last bite
Before landing in Red Rock bay[3]

No money, no food, no drink
Just a coconut and half a kumara[4]
His skeleton sailors crawl up the beach
To rest under a pohutukawa[5] tree

A sigh left their mouths
Moving hairs from their forehead
Watching footprints on the sand
As they listen to her song

A mermaid from Hawaiki[6]
Sitting naked on the rocks
Filling the air with sweet sounds
On Kupe's ear and his men

They grew stronger with each note
Muscles and tendons gaining strength
They lift their spirits, body and clubs
And conquered the land of the moa[7].

---

1. Maori name for New Zealand
2. Kupe was the first Maori to land in New Zealand according to Maori legends
3. A beach in Wellington where Kupe landed according to legends
4. Sweet potato in Maori
5. *Metrosideros excelsa* (scientific name)
6. Ancestral land of the Polynesians according to legend
7. An ancient giant flightles bird in New Zealand

MAUI'S PILLOW

He pulled the islands
From the deep
Using a magic hook and line
That he got from the sky

Te Ika a Maui[1]
Was the next find
Miata[2] and the mermaids

Held up the time

The fish jumped higher
Than the clouds
Causing bumps on Aoraki[3]
At the front of the boat

Finally he fell asleep
Tangaroa[4] got some sheep
To keep him warm in his dreams
Of his pillow the angels keep.

---

1. The Maori name for the North Island of New Zealand
2. A character from the book 'The children of the Gods' by Semisi Pone
3. The Maori Name for Mt Cook in the South Island of New Zealand
4. One of the Polynesian Gods

ANCIENT KINGDOM

Tuheitia[1] is the King
Whakapapa[2] from Kupe
Whanau[3], mokopuna's[4], wings
Long distance, waka[5] and Kupe

Looks like skeletons
From the past

Under tattered sails
That may not last

Hawaiki songs of ancestors
Leading warriors home
Seafarers forgot the stars
And ended up in Rome

A small village in Porirua[6]
Pa[7] guarded by spirits
Marae[8] orators, not dons
Run the iwi[9], collect rates.

---

1. Maori King
2. Maori Genealogy
3. Maori Children
4. Maori grand-children
5. Maori boat or canoe
6. A suburb of Wellington
7. A Maori fort
8. A Maori village or meeting house
9. Maori extended family

NAPOLEON I

A soldier from Corsica[1]
With seven siblings
He became the Emperor
They became Kings

Constantly at war
With his neighbors
Remarried Marie[2] of Austria
Won battles with Prussia[3]

Initiator of laws
And public structures
Lost at Waterloo[4]
Exiled to Elba[5]

Back for 100 days
And lost again
This time exiled to St Helens[6]
Where he passed away.

---

1. Corsica – an island in the Mediterranean off the coast
    of France where Napoleon Bonaparte I was born.
2. Marie of Austria – Princess Marie of Austria was
    Napoleon Bonaparte I's second wife. His first wife
    Josephine did not bear him any children. He married
    Princess Marie of Austria and they had a son,
    Napoleon Bonaparte II.
3. Prussia – the former Kingdom of Prussia which is
    now the German Republic.
4. Waterloo – the battle of Waterloo made the Duke of
    Wellington famous for giving Napoleon Bonaparte I
    his first taste of defeat in battle.
5. Elba – an island off the coast of Italy and Corsica
    where Napoleon Bonaparte I lived when he abdicated
    in 1814-15.

6. St Helens or St Helena – an island in the South
    Atlantic where Napoleon Bonaparte I lived when he
    lost again....after the 100 days...he escaped from
    Elba and seized power in Paris for 100 days.

SAMSON[1]

A strongman with long hair
Whom Delilah drove to despair
By cutting it short
The bidding of her lords

Blinded by his love for a woman
Who did not care
He was as strong as Iron man
As brave as a bear

During the feast of his enemies
In the largest building in the land
He received divine inspiration
A plan for his revenge

Take me to the strongest pillars
He said to the wee lad
I will destroy the killers
And the boy was glad

He shook the building
With his mighty arms

And it collapsed like an inkling
On that fateful farm.

---

1. The story of Samson in the bible

OTTO

Otto means wealth
Attar is stealth
Essential oils
Squeezed from a rose

Known as the Great
Seized power in 912
Became King of the Germans
Holy Roman Emperor too

Maintained supreme power
Over Italy and European tribes
Send Christians over
To Scandinavia and Slavonic sides

Inventor of the four stroke engine
Known as the Otto cycle
Which make many machines
Run smoothly like a bible

Ottoman Empire
Soldiers for hire
Started by a Sultan
In 1345.

PAU[1]

He welcomed Captain James Cook
Who just came to have a look
What is that fancy hair?
It's just to impress her
The headdress[2] is made of feathers
Just during fine weather

When the King's concubines
Are paraded in a line
He will choose one for tonight
And give the rest to the seamen
Captain James Cook will choose first
And his sailors can have the rest

Their descendants are still there
Their business is hunting whales
But that was banned by convention
And they have to look for a job
To look after themselves
Modern decisions on ancient mariners

Magazines wrote their story
Of the explorer's descendants
Who look just like the seafarer
But a bit brown on the skin
Leaving the sea was hard
Tilling the land and money earners.

---

1. The 36th Tu'i Tonga
2. The famous head-dress is known as the 'Palatavake' it is in the museum in Vienna, Austria according to some reports.

THE KAVA[1] CIRCLE

The King's kava circle
Sat at the village grounds
Investing an important title
On their chief's crown

The first cup is for the king
Filled with kava and poison[2]
He died for many generations
From his enemies murderous feelings

Revenge and hatred of centuries
Kill the King and his family
To restore the pride of his clan
Through the kava circle

Man is a weak and fragile creature
Brains deteriorating and weaker
Push harder and he explodes
A time bomb with no heart

Lo'au³ was a Spanish sailor
Who shared his travel experience
From shared kava in Micronesia
And stories in Santo⁴.

---

1. *Piper methysticum* (scientific name)
2. A reference to assassinations by poisoning in ancient times
which require the King's talking Chief to drink his cup in case
it may be poisoned.
3. The man attributed with the preparation of the kava
beverage in Tonga. It is possible he may have been a European
sailor who picked up the kava drinking habit from other
islands in the Pacific.
4. An island in Vanuatu. Vanuatu Islands have the most
kava species in the Pacific region.

MAUI'S WAKA AND FISH

Maui went fishing in his waka
He didn't own a car
Then caught a fish
But it was bigger than his boat
He had to let it go
It was just for a show

Lucky for the Kiwis
And their Iwis
His fish made them rich
From all the pigs
Running around on its back
Then they build some sheds
And stayed in one but rent the rest
For several centuries
They have collected money
And restored his waka
But Maui liked the other
Which was a yacht
That he bought
Went sailing around the countries
Lasting for centuries.

17. POEMS ABOUT WRITING

THE WISDOM OF A BOOK

Some stories for a kid
Wrapped in a good quality book
To inspire a greater dream
Than those of this generation

Books last forever, stories never die
Like Homer's Iliad and Odyssey
Inspiring a thousand generations

Stories of Gods, demons and men

The feijoa tree and the spaceship
Rala the alien and the dog looking cat [1]
Taniwha's in Northcote and a Prince's bride [1]
Characters in my stories for my son

But he grew up too quickly
He is too old for my stories
Now more useful for a grandchild
Who's just turning five.

---

1. Characters from my short stories

MY BUSINESS

I wrote a book
To sell for money
But the internet is full
Of billions of goods

I made a little cash
From high price sales
Then I added discounts
And sold nothing!

I put up my mark-up
To make it worthwhile

Small profits from knowledge
Must result in appreciation

Technology must work
In the age of information
Not just hard labor
And selling my time

I do a lot of good
With my writing business
Books for the needy
Poems for the wise

When I make some money
I will travel the world
A backpack and a computer
To write a song and story

A legacy for my children
Grand-children and fans
Who like to smile and enjoy
My meandering verses.

A WRITER'S FORTUNE

I love writing
Articles, stories, poems
But I still have no m's

The big m is scarce when you write
Just like fishing there's no bite
They say writers are poor
Like fishing there's no lure
They only earn $14,000 per year
Writers command the rear
One day I will make some money
Like a bear seeking honey
Once a year, I'll be lucky
Only a hermit knows
The highs and the lows
As Bob Dylan sings
It's blowing in the wind
The answer is in the win
Buy a lotto ticket
It might get you out of the thicket
A hermit's bush
Keep me out of the sun
I am having fun
I hope I don't lose
My sanity like a moose
During the winter
Which is not kinder
I think like a writer
Act like a tiger
Meals like manna
Surviving like a soldier
During the war

His body full of sores
He dreams of his youth
Wealthy and uncouth
One day I will record
What happened
For the Lords
Oh how, I will pay a fortune
For a cider
To calm me down like a writer.

A WRITER'S TALE

They say books earn more from exports
Than making wine
I have stories of sorts
Invite my neighbors to dine

To share and write these tales
Like Odysseus, sailors in a gale
In search of his land and family
Books to educate you and me

Blessed is the man who can write
If all is lost, words can fight
They last for a thousand generations
And fill millions with motivation

Invest your money in the right place

Productive people can win the race
They can turn a little money
Into goods, services and pots of honey

Don't be a fool
And throw it to the wolves
It's just a big hole
Be courageous, clever and bold.

THE OLD MASTERS

The Lady of the Lake[1]
And The Wind[2] remind me
Of the beauty of words
Rhyme of the Ancient Mariner[3]

An Ode to a Grecian Urn[4]
Light bulb moment for a child
Learning English literature
Language of the old masters

Shakespeare, Stevenson, Twain
Scott, Shelly, Coleridge
Keats, Byron and me
Rhymes of an Aspiring Writer[5].

---

1. A Poem by Sir Walter Scott
2. A poem by Robert Louis Stevenson
3. A poem by Samuel Taylor Coleridge

18. POEMS ABOUT SHAPES

MY FAMILY TREE

First there
Was Adam and Eve
Then there were holes like a sieve
Through countless generations just like an equation
I have to look through genealogies like a book
But finally I managed to work out
Who belongs in which line, like pines
In a forest, tidy with no mess
Now I can have a rest
My children, grandchildren
Can read without a sheet
Where they come
From like a book
And commit
To their
Memory
Who
Is
In
The
Family Tree.

UPSIDEDOWN BOOT

I went to Italy with a Kiwi
He said I am from Buller
My dad was the ruler
Of our town
Yes it's a noun
We are real
Let's deal
We won
The rugby
On a buggy
With plenty
Of balls
On a roll
But here
In Rome
Lost comb
In the rush
To the bus
Come on
Driver
Just look
At the map
My good chap.

19. POEMS ABOUT HISTORY

TREATY OF WAITANGI

The powers of Europe required colonies
British, French, Spanish, German, Portuguese
Seeking new land to expand their industries
Gold mining, spice trading and planting trees
Farming, whaling, livestock and fisheries

They raced through Africa, Far East, Caribbean
Near East, Middle East, China and Japan
Every kind of trade, there's money to be earned
Then they came to the islands of the Pacific
Australia and New Zealand to raise some sheep

The British were very successful
In building infrastructure and trading tools
Getting everyone to obey the rules
Africa, Far East, Caribbean and the Pacific
In New Zealand they negotiated a treaty

The Treaty of Waitangi[1] it was called
To achieve peace and equality for all
But it was a bit like Animal Farm
Some animals were more equal than others
The Maoris were a bit sore, they can't resort to war

The Crown agreed to settle their grievances
Over the way settlers moved their fences
After 100 years it's hard to return the land
Which has improved their power to earn
They gave back billions, they understand

Every Iwi must submit a claim
Keeping the peace is the Crown's aim
$150 million here, $750 million there
For the Tangata Whenua[1] to share
And to invest for their children's care

Now the settlements seem to work
Most offers by the Crown they accept
Both sides seem to agree
It's important for their families
It's men of goodwill working for peace

And the country grows in prosperity
When all citizens agree
To work for the good of all
So their civilization will never fall
And perish like the Gauls.

---

1. Waitangi is the place in Northland, New Zealand where the treaty was signed.

20. POEMS ABOUT SELF-IMPROVEMENT

WE ARE ALL MILLIONAIRES[1]

I have 104,000 hours to sell
It's worth one million dollars
If one hour is worth $10
Sell half to invest
And live on the rest

In Australia, one hour is worth more
Invest two million
And be richer than before
Donate a dollar to the United Nations
Make 350 billion for foreign relations

There will be no poverty
All nations will be rich
We all pay for our uses
All sweet, no abuse
Go for a holiday
Smile all the way

In Africa there's no rain
Water the crops from the tap
Tow a few icebergs there
And fill the tanks to the brim
No problems, sing some hymns

There are no problems
In our wonderful world
Only pirates and their girls
Leaving skeletons in every cupboard
The wishes of their lords

They do not wish
To make you rich
Only slaves in their schemes
It gives their small brains power
To see you in pain and suffer

More money are in the hands
Of a few rich people
Than all the population of Africa
They do not want solutions
Only disease, death and pollution.

---

1. - This is also the title of a book about self-worth by Semisi
Pone. Available from amazon.com

THINK LIKE A MAN

Act like a lady, think like a man
So put a ring on her hand
But he ran a mile
As soon as she smiled

Act like a lady, think like a man
So put a chainsaw in her hand
That was a birthday present
From her management

Act like a lady, think like a man
Build a house on her land
Then he divorced her
As soon as he got his share

Act like a lady, think like a man
Watch the footprints on the sand
There are only two
Just left and right.

LOSING WEIGHT

My mates like to sing
While dancing in the ring
Climb the mountain, be bold
And avoid catching a cold

You might see lots of planets
Like they do on the internet
But getting off your butt
Is a plan and a must

Go to Guatemala
And plant some kumara
Just like a scientist
Discovering frogs leap!

Your lower back
Can carry the bag
Make sure your visa
Notes from the teacher

If you can run a mile
Together with a smile
Just do it yourself
Stop acting like a girl

As long as it's working
Bonus points or just checking
Farmers chore is not a bore
Lose weight and not so sore.

21. POEMS ABOUT WORLD LEADERS

BARACK OBAMA FOR PRESIDENT[1].

He was a lawyer from Chicago
Who was educated at Harvard
He earned everything he's got
Not a silver spoon, he worked hard

A shining example of the American ideal
Why millions emigrated to America
Work hard, learn hard, practice away
You may be President some day

It was the American dream
Bring Auntie, Uncle, Papa, Nana, to work
They emigrated to become millionaires
Buy a house and grow their roots there

President Obama is proof
That the American dream is real
You do not have to be white and rich
To occupy the Oval Office

The whole world applauds America
For showing such conviction
I am sure they will go far
To realize all their dreams

Vote Obama in again
For another 4 years, a second term
To show the world you are mature
It's not about race, that's for sure

He came through like a shining light
Beating recession and war without a fight
Displaying lessons in respect and dignity

Barack Obama is the President for me.

QUEEN ELIZABETH'S DIAMOND JUBILEE

She was crowned in 1953
Salote III was our Queen
She traveled to London for the coronation
And got caught in her roofless car in the rain
Noel Coward made a comment
Which has resulted in much lament
About Emperor Haille Selassie
Who was sitting by her side
Typical English, somebody said
Queen Elizabeth is not like that
She came to Tonga in 1970
My grandfather was sick with the flu
He got up and cleaned his lawn
And waited in his Sunday best by the road
So he can wave at the Queen when she passed
With his crutch by his side
I was only 8 years old
And I watched my grandfather as he strode
It must have been my imagination
The pride and joy of a nation
I saw the Queen's car stop

The Queen had a word with my Pop
And I thought she was tops.

22. POEMS ABOUT LAW AND INJUSTICE

MY CONVICTIONS.

When I was sixteen
I was a typical teen
I went to the shopping center
And got attacked by some gangsters

I had to fight for my life
Even one brought his wife
Luckily I know a punch or two
Or would be black and blue

Then the policeman came
I got all the blame
I got a ticket
Judged and convicted

It happened many times
My Dad asked me why
I said I don't know
I was feeling a bit low

It seems the policeman
Got a call from the gangsters
To catch us fighting
A frame or just a game

Now I have to leave the country
Only dope smokers get money for free
I'll get a job overseas
And realize my dreams.

STATE HOTEL

It's a prison hotel
They make so well
Many who go there
Never want to return

Free housing, free food
They never had it so good
Free training, free entertainment
It's a huge compliment

It's hard on the outside
They have to work all day
In the hotel, inside
Just sleep, showers and play

When they get released
They commit another crime
To be in trouble with the Police
And return to prison with a smile.

THE PRISONS

It's a huge expense
To house criminals and their friends
Just leave them at home
Detention, just let it be known

Fine the lawbreakers
More money for government coffers
But still uphold their rights
Or get ready for a fight

The worst ones
Need their heads fixed
There is a defect in their brains
It's not just a trick

Send them to an asylum
They are just too dumb
Give them some pills
To smarten their wills

Now we are all happy
Save money, make money
Just make it snappy
No more torture, clean not dirty.

THE LAW

In 1753, they hang thieves from the nearest tree
They run and become outlaws to be free
Even if you did nothing wrong
But swayed the women with your songs
They will still shoot you dead
With a bullet to the head

Then the Evangelists
Gave the law a new twist
Love thy neighbor as thyself
The teachings of Christ is your wealth
Uphold the rights of the poor
And feed the hungry at every door

The University took it up
And discussed it in every pub
Logic, philosophy and psychology
A mixture of the knowledge tree
It's not only religion that counts
But philosophical morals do the rounds

Plato, Socrates and Aristotle
The original proponents of the morals
Every scholar in Ancient Greece
Discussed ways to keep the peace
It was the responsibility of the State
To uphold its citizens rights

The Lawyers of to-day
Only work for their pay
They won't put up a fight
If your payment does not suffice
It's up to the learned Judge
If he wants to uphold your rights.

BUSH JUSTICE

There are 5 million criminals
In our country
They thought it's just trivial
To let one million live in the bush for free

Many were convicted when they were ten
Outcasts, Outlaws in their land
They get tortured for a lifetime
For suffering from too much wine

The Conviction System is our torture machine
We'll punish you 1000 times we'll win

They don't know it's illegal
To treat people that way, even criminals

My friend apologized
He does not know why
I'm sorry it's so hard
Our legal people didn't go to Harvard

Only a wise man would know
The law can be a cruel blow
It it's in the wrong hands
They'll never learn.

23. POEMS ABOUT MIGRATION

A   MIGRANT'S DREAM.

I am an Islander who came from asunder
I overstayed in New Zealand because I have no land
I ran away from Immigration Officials
I am regarded as a criminal
But one day I will get my PR[1]
If only I can marry RR[2]
My uncle saved me
I slept under his tree
It is better he says
Stay here during the days
Then the neighbors reported me

So I left again
Now I have to pay where ever I stay
Finally I got a boat and hid in its load
I thought it was going to Australia
But ended up in Antarctica
Now my back is frozen
My head is still tolerant
Of the cold and my freezing hole
I think it's better in Heaven
So I let my soul go at seven
And met St Peter's mate at heaven's gate
St Peter said "You can't overstay here.
You have to go back to the tavern"
Then I woke up and found
I passed out in the pub.

---

1. Permanent Residence
2. Rachel Ray

THE RIGHT CHOICE

Professionals come to New Zealand
They say it's the right choice
Their business never break even
And leave they have no voice

Those left behind, is like running blind
Getting funds is like digging mines

It might explode, no one knows
There's nothing to borrow

Funds are scarce
It's the economic crisis
We know it's a farce
Just the increasing prices

Government officials complain
Shortage of money is the problem
But still spend billions
On non-productive people

Artists, writers and new business
Bring in billions of dollars
But never make ends meet
They are broke but still scholars

They try to make a living
Writing books or start singing
But never make anything
Dope smokers and oldies get all the funding

Then Gareth Morgan, millionaire kiwi
Proposed the Universal Basic Income[1]
For all struggling self-employed
And underfunded businesses

He is barking mad, says John Key[2]
We propose more jobs, says Andrew Little[3]
Only the Germans are smarter
They top up wages 30 years ago[4].

---

1. The UBI is a proposal by Kiwi millionaire, Gareth Morgan, and others to help support under-funded businesses and self-employed people with Government paid 'allowance'.
2. Prime Minister of New Zealand and leader of the National Party
3. Leader of the Labor Party in New Zealand
4. German expatriates working overseas whose income was lower than German salaries were 'topped up' by the German Government to meet German standards. There is, at least, one confirmed case known to the author.

24. POEMS ABOUT WORLD PROBLEMS

OIL

It is the Black Gold
A product of dinosaurs
And plants of old
Squeezed by tonnes of pressure
Underneath the Earth
Into oily matter
Discovered by man
To make billions from his land
It exploded the age of machines
And made some men

As rich as the Queen

The middle east countries became rich
And turned the sand into properties
Shell, Exxon and BP
Were the big three
They controlled oil around the world
And caused wars to drill their wells
Then the oil countries hit back
They formed OPEC
Now there's a balance of power
They got the control tower

They punished the world in guise
By raising their price
Which caused havoc in the USA
Nixon announced his dismay
Petrol is short, stay home for a day
Until we can sort out the blame
IRAQ invaded Kuwait
It was another Watergate

The second war was worse than before
After 911 they invaded again
Osama Bin Laden was to blame
Citizens of Iraq complain
Despite our tonnes of oil we are still short
We blame the Americans and the war

They came here and took our oil
Saddam's gold, cash and the spoils
Kuwait is a different story
They now live in multi-stories

In Kuwait they were poor
Then heaven opened up its door
Now they are richer than everyone
Their people are having fun
The oil trade is back to normal
Now the seven sisters in control
They got rid of Gaddafi, Saddam and Bin Laden
And all the fly by nights
Their soldiers are always ready for a fight
To uphold what is right.

25. POEMS ABOUT PLANTS AND FLOWERS

THE FLOWER

It bursts out of itself
As if to breath air
Opening petals
Of brilliant colors
Attracting man and animals

Its beautiful scent
Admired by millions

Kings, Queens and royals
But only a bee knows
Its sweet nectar

As the sun rises
Its brilliance is enhanced
Bees feed, man agree
Only to sigh when it wilts
With the setting of the sun.

THE ORANGE TREE

It fruits every year
Branches bending with orange
Children delight in picking
And enjoying its sweet juice

Then one day a tiny insect
Landed on one leaf
Probed and sucked its juice
Then left leaving a virus

The viruses took over
The cells in the leaves
Producing more illness
Wilt and yellowing leaves

In a month, its leaves
Were all dry and gone
Just a skeleton of branches
Where once was a beautiful tree

The kids cried, the orange tree died
Of a mysterious illness
Not knowing it was an insect
Which brought the deadly disease

The orange tree was chopped down
And used for firewood
The kids cried again
No more sweet fruits.

COCONUT.

It's the most useful tree
In the tropical countries
Weave the leaves for housing
Or a basket for carrying

Drink or eat the fruit
Make a fish trap from the roots
The trunk can provide timber
Firewood, medicine or cinder

Make wine from the flowers
Oil provide shampoo for your shower
Leaf spines make a broom
Young leaves for mats in your room

Make desiccated coconut from the meat
Fill the cream in boxes and heat
Export to overseas markets
Improved earnings is the target

The fiber and the shell
Support pot plants on the shelf
Make ropes and buttons
And load them by the carton

Use the lamina for making toys
Or fishing baskets for the boys
Medicine from young fruits
You can create all sorts of goods

Coconuts are secondary colonizers
In all new beaches and islands
It floats on the ocean like markers
On the sand it sprouts in a month.

TANE MAHUTA[1]

A majestic giant kauri[2]
Covered with epiphytes
A colossal column among trees
Silent, awesome, lord of the forest

Tane Mahuta was standing here
One thousand years before Kupe
And it has been standing here
One thousand years since
Timeless guardian of the land

If only I could climb
Its wall-like trunk
To enjoy the views from above
Of Rimu[3], Totara[4], Pohutukawa[5]

Ancient, quiet, beautiful
Different colored canopy
Of birds and native trees
Songs of forgotten dreams

An ancient story for my children
Of nature's beauty and might
A mighty tree from a tiny seed
Once silently falling
In the dead of night.

1. A giant kauri in Northland, New Zealand. It means 'Lord of the Forest' in Maori according to many reports. Its age is estimated at 1500–2,000 years.
2. *Agathis australis* (scientific name)
3. *Dacrydium cupressinum* (scientific name)
4. *Podocarpus totara* (scientific name)
5. *Medrosideros excelsa* (scientific name)

ROSES AND DAISY

They must be flowers of the Gods
Dewdrops shining on petals
At sunrise they look like diamonds
Strings on pink, white and red

Birds sing their praises
Flying in search of worms
Or honey in the garden
Covered in marigold and roses

Cympidiums of red, yellow and purple
Complement the stand of roses
Therapy for the eyes and soul
On a quiet morning before dawn

A rare geranium with large pink flowers
Found in a corner flanked with daisy

Blue and white petals of beauty
Picture perfect harmony

A vibrant growth of plants
Flowers and dark green leaves
Abundant with birds and bees
Stimulating my senses and brain.

THE LAWN

Specks of white and globes of yellow
Daisies coming to life mixed in dandelions
Nightshade clumps colonizing our lawn
Where a concrete pathway disturbed the soil

Nut grass appearance like a newcomer
Looking tall like coconuts among leucaena[1]
Broad leaved docks are all gone
Sprayed with intent and weedkiller

Creeping oxalis appear after rain
A dark green blotch on daisy white
Large leaved plantain becoming scarce
My management recipe on the lawn

Now it looks like a carpet
Fit for a king and the children
To roll in, sleep and play

A worthwhile exercise for me.

---

1. A small tree usually classified as a weed in many countries. *Leucaena leucocephala* or *Leucaena glauca* (Scientific Name).

26. POEMS ABOUT MORALS

MORALS

The Old Testament says a tooth for a tooth
The Koran says stone the adulterous woman
But the New Testament needs proof
Before you slap her suspected man

Philosophers argue dignity and respect
Is what you need to reflect
Immanuel Kant's immortal words
You don't need to kill to be bad

If everyone tell a malicious lie
You probably feel it's better to die
Your world will come crumbling down
Everyone thinks you are not genuine

King Solomon is a wise man
When he decided she is bad
To ask for half her neighbor's baby

Without a care for the mother's sanity

Judges decide your fate
Based on what you did on the date
Whether you decided to rob or not to rob
If you planned to do the job

They argue the case of the battered wife
Was she right to take the husband's life
What do you do when you are black and blue
Take her to the women's refuge

Human rights are more important
Than her terrible crime
She did not plan to kill
She just wanted to survive

She is lucky the judge learned philosophy
And the logic of motives
If it was in the third world
She will hang from the nearest tree

Philosophers, church ministers
The jury, judge and officers
Are seen to promote the truth
The Crown has the burden of proof

Adam and Eve didn't know they were naked
Until she decided to taste it
The fruit of good and bad
With no right to be heard.

27. POEMS ABOUT HEALTH

DEPRESSION

Depression, that's my impression
No dollars, no sex, no aggression
No food, no job only alcohol
Every woman looks like a doll

Depression, that's my impression
Just a big hole on my section
No tree, no shrub only stones
Hopefully they're diamonds

Depression, that's my impression
Mental patients with affection
Just give them some pills
They'll wave from the window sills

Depression, that's my impression
Get a massage is my selection
Just rub me all over
A relaxation exercise for lovers.

28. POEMS ABOUT ECONOMICS AND COMMERCE

MARKETING

We sell books everyday
An advance to write a way
To start a business on a shoestring
If there's no job to reach your dream

Write another book
We'll take a look
And pay you half
With royalties for your part

There are millions to be made
Just workout what's the date
To launch our next project
It's as fast as a rocket

A thousand books to my name
In 15 years that's my claim
Books last a million years
Yarns that move the world to tears.

THE CUSTOMER

The customer is king
In my business
Whether he be rich with power
Or poor with no assets

He pays for the cost
The profits and development
Services must equal
The amount of his payments

Competition cannot lure him
He is loyal and supportive
The customer knows the value
Of a good service received.

TAX

Give money to Caesar
And your husband, not Jesus
Spirits in a cadaver
Moving robots of flesh

Working for families
Made by wise politicians
Sweet smelling rose and lilies
For kids food, fees, expense, linen

Reimbursements of over payment
Compensation for illness
Book keeping entries by government
Robbers, villains and Princes

Outstanding pay from SPC
Made by foreign affairs
Consultancy and publication fees
Concubines and diplomatic lawyers

A salary of two million
For the past twenty years
Unlimited sick leave
Received under the table.

29. POEMS ABOUT POVERTY

POVERTY

When I was young
We lived in town
All the food was made of flour
Rice and sugar by the hour

In the villages, they had fruit
Yams, pigs, chicken and seafood
There was money from the tourists
Crops, melons and fishing

My Dad worked for the government
We were considered rich
A large house, windows and a fridge
Cooking with electricity and kerosene

He made $60 per fortnight
A high salary in government
But buying power was weak
Only free buses with no car

Every Sunday we had 'umu
Rootcrops, rawfish and meat in lu[1]
Pawpaw , watermelon, mangoes
Immersed in coconut cream

During Christmas I had toys
And roasted pig with the boys
Camp in the church hall
And eat till you burst

Then I went overseas
They say we are poor
We sleep under trees
And fish with no lure

Kiwi kids go to school
With no proper lunch
Refuse to obey the rules

No food stunts their minds

Billions of dollars
Are spent on the roads
Laborers not scholars
Whiskey to warm their throats.

Training workers is their choice
Deeds with no voice
Brains from supervisors
Smoking marijuana for a break

A Police State
In the making
Dictators in secret
Everyone needs money

Poverty exists
In the mind
Read Oliver Twist[2]
Dickens[3] is more fun

It's what people do
That makes a difference
Lock your kids in the loo
Or become friends

Empowering people is the aim
Use skills to solve problems
When you have nothing
Be more creative

Convert the sand into oil
Plant taro instead of corn
Protein and vitamin from the leaves
Carbohydrate from the corm

Don't eat steaks everyday
Try fried rice with eggs
It's a quarter of the cost
The same value for less

Plant your own vegetables
To save money
Drink three beers
Instead of twenty

Your wealth is in your brain
It controls your body
And keep you sane
Train it to be ready

Nothing is worth more
Than yourself
Treat it with respect

Always save time to reflect.

---

1. A Tongan delicacy made of meat, onion and coconut cream wrapped in taro leaves.
2. Oliver Twist – one of the famous novels by Charles Dickens
3. Dickens – Charles Dickens a famous British writer in the 19th century

THE BUSKER

Singing is her profession
And playing musical instruments
Fans stand at attention
She has many friends

Traveling the country
Villages, cities and the world
Singing to all and sundry
Playing the guitar so well

At the end of each day
She counts her earnings
One hundred dollars for today
Or just a few coins

It is a good earner
She writes and paints as a learner
What's all that complaint

About unemployment?.
THESE WERE THE DAYS

Tommy was a laborer
Earning $11 per hour
It was the highest pay
He could command in those days

Working for families[1]
Gave him $500 for his children
Every week for shopping
There were ten of them

It was the best policy
Of the Labor Government[2]
Assistance for the needy
Intervention where it counts

Then he won the lotto
A trick by the Police
365[3] reasons to leave town
And come back for another round.

---

1. Working for families – was a financial support system
    established by the Labor Government of New
    Zealand under Helen Clark (1999–2008). Payments
    to low income families every week were based on the
    number of children under 18 years of age.

2. Labor Government – Labor Government, New Zealand under Ms Helen Clark from 1999 to 2008.
3. 365 – the number of the Police Station on Glenfield Road in Glenfield, Auckland, New Zealand.

STREET PROFESSIONAL

He was a professional
Earning $100,000 a year
He lost his family and job
And could not afford a beer

After years of looking
Moved to the street
Living under bridges
Shattered dream of riches

They searched for him for years
No address, no phone, no email
Finally meeting in tears
Moss grew on his nails

Years of inactivity
Drove him crazy
He thinks like a pro
But talks like a mute.

30. POEMS ABOUT DREAMS AND IMAGINATION

DREAMTIME

Let's go walkabout
Find medicinal trees
Ancient cures for love

Let's stand on one foot
For the next 1,000 years
Aboriginal faith in boots

Let's swim the length
Of the Murray river
Show everyone our strength

Let's donate the Barrier Reef
To humankind
Queensland for raising beef

Let's catch a rainbow
For our children
Dream time cures for sorrow

 Let's find the trade winds
To power our boats
Unlimited Energy

Let's harness the moon
For a field trip
To Pluto and come back soon

Let's hold the melting ice
In Antarctica and the Arctic
Saving mankind is the price

Let's replant the trees
In the Sahara
Our gift to Africa

Let's love each other
For the next billion years
A moment to God
But a long time in beers.

BROKEN DREAMS

I dream of being rich
And end up a pauper
I dream of being King
But only changed a diaper

Many people are lost
In the land of broken dreams
Singing songs of Babylon[1]
Under trees by the stream

They long for a cruise
On the QEII[2]
See the islands of paradise
Antarctica too

Keep sailing to the east
Throw the fishing line
Catch a shark's dream
And eat them alive

Then become a star
In somebody else's dream
You will go far
Singing Babylon by the stream.

---

1. Babylon - one of the famous countries or cities in the
   Bible…probably part of ancient Persia which is
   present day Iran.
2. QEII – the cruise liner Queen Elizabeth II

GENEALOGY

Rivers of blood
Run in my veins
Genes not Noah's flood
From my parents
Chromosomes and parts
From ancient Gods

And divine plans

Empires build with brains
Knights from distant shores
Muscles produce grains
Tradition and folklores
Navigate the stormy seas
And fishing albacores

Will of iron made in the land
Of fairies, spirits and fierce warriors
Kings, Queens, farmers and fishermen
Traits so precious like hours
Forever lost, new things to learn
I am, the total product of my ancestors.

THE SUN

It floats in space
Trillions of gigaphotons
Stationary, but winner of the race
Chloroplast, green leaf, neurons

Stars twinkling in the dark
Prophets of the Messiah
Energy packages on an ark
Feeding the world's survivors

One side of a boat
Great wall of China
The sun releases its load
To feed mankind, science finders.

INDIGO CHIEF

Prince of the Rainbow people
Oil on stormy seas
Medicine for a cripple
Degrees of life and laws
Hungry for a tipple
Fierce warrior like jaws

Swearer of the young bathrooms
Banana bundles on a breadfruit
Put the enemy on a broom
Lover of all that is good
Traveler from the Pacific to Khartoum
On a jetplane, canoe on a boot

Yam planter on the wind
Fruits of the islands
On a sacred stream
Flying foxes on a banyan
Property of mangoes to clean
A house of bricks to finance

Mountain, south of neighbors
Polls of opinions, war at night
Enjoys hard work and labor
Till dark with no light
Wit as sharp as a saber
When kava drinkers need a fight

Four x's in a matter
Like atoms in the blood
Prince of heads in a letter
Earned cash like a flood
Score goals like a header
Found a fish in the guts

Successful water flows
Love for ancient shores
Memories fly high and low
Migrating tuna and albacores
Fishermen from the wind
Collect their brother to resume.

THE SHOW

Jump from space
Break the speed of sound
Take Lennox Lewis[1]
Through another round

Bomb the twin towers
And start a war
Eat $1 trillion dollars
Like a hungry boar

Go to Hollywood
And create a movie
Lord of the Rings[2], Avatar[3]
Jaws[4], Dinosaurs, The Conqueror

Run for President
Of your country
Import some voters
Sex for free

Become King of the World
In the new order
United Nations with no borders
Or migrate to Jupiter

Convert the sea
Into oil
Save the world
And the collect the spoils

---

1. Lennox Lewis – British boxer who unified the WBC,
    WBA and IBA boxing titles when he became the
    undisputed heavyweight boxing champion of the
    world during the early 2000s.

2. Lord of the Rings – a series of movies by Peter Jackson of New Zealand based on the book by JRRTolkien.
3. Avatar – a movie by James Cameron, also from New Zealand!
4. Jaws – a movie about a great white shark that was attacking people.

EMOTIONS

Held together by bones
And seventy percent of water
Tough skin made of scones
And brains like Chaucer[1]

Nerve communicate thoughts
Electrical impulses
Made and signed by God
Enhanced feelings like spices

Rays from the sun
Caught by chloroplast
Turned into carbohydrate and rum
Food energy that last

ATP[2] move muscles
Political decisions in Brussels
Photons of intervention
From angels and conventions

I think therefore I am
Existence by conclusion
Like the sacrificial lamb
Exercises in oblivion

Are emotions made of H_2O?
Intelligence like water flows
Or ATP, genes and photons?
Held together by protons

A cadaver is a body
Devoid of life
What makes it move?
And emotional like a wife?

There are more mysteries
On heaven and earth
Than your philosophies
A universe for nerds.

---

1. A monk and writer in early English history
2. Adenosine triphosphate is an energy rich compound that
feed the tissues in animals

GREEN WISDOM

Bond of the wise man
Books for a dollar
Inspiration for children

Ordinary men become scholars

Save the earth from death
Dying environments, dirty air
A beautiful woman on a bed
Loving tears like a river

Color of life and plants
Oxygen for the planet
Try to breath but can't
Consequences, industrial dirt

Supplanter of faith
Disciple of the world
Lover of life
And a beautiful girl.

THE GLOBAL CITIZEN

First Emperor of China
In the age of Dragons
Commanded demons not warriors
To conquer King Solomon

As wise an an ant
As strong as steel
Numerous as the sand
Supporting thousands of reefs

King of the Vikings
In the age of sorcerers
Commanded knights and Merlin
Guidance of the wanderers

Powerful as the earth
Which provide support
Holding armies in his hands
Commander of the Lords

President of the United States
In the space and nuclear age
Determines policy, ruler of fate
Director of people, wiser than a sage

Secretary General of the United Nations
In the World Government
Determines the destiny
Of everyone under the firmament

Chancellor of the world
In the new order
Agreed by all governments
Countries with no borders.

EMMA - PRINCESS OF DREAMS

A beautiful girl

With glasses
An old woman
Who like molasses

Princess in the shadow
Of the twilight guards
Who swung her bow
And shot a passing dove

Lived in the mystery
Of traditions and legends
Fairies of Pulotu
Angels of heaven

A royal warrior maiden
Of the South Seas
Emblem of the family
Lost in history

Mermaid of lush Hawaiki
Ancestral land of the Polynesian
Singing songs of the sirens
To guide the war Kalias back

In the court of King Arthur
She owns the round table
And holds indestructible Excalibur[1]
For Sir Lancelot to follow

Sails of the Vikings
Thor[2] and Zeus[3]
Gave fire to Maui[4]
Tongan Prometheus[5]

Rules the world's seas
From the sky
Speaks in thunder
Travels the waves in style.

---

1. The famous sword of King Arthur in the story of 'King Arthur'
2. A Scandinavian God
3. Father of the Gods in Greek
4. A Polynesian God
5. A Titan who stole fire from the Gods to help mankind in Greek mythology.

THE MINISTER

Messenger of God
Chief before the Lords
Grandchild of Kings
Angels gave him wings

Joseph was number one
Julia, not Mary, was his wife
Childless in a manger

An LDS[1] manager
The second Bonaparte[2]
Succeeded at Lourde's
Became emperor of his day
Soldier, Commander, prayer

Far, far away
Thy bible in storyland
Moe[3] in Simpson's bar
Man U[4] champions of soccer

See sherpa's mighty guardian
Of the eight golden fleece
Himalayas of ancient Greece
In the sands, under Lifuka's[4] trees

Charlotte, princess in disguise
Apollo and Aphrodite to devise
Partners, queen, empires
Centuries came, time flies

The island's still there
William Mariner's[5] story bared
How they lived and died
During the civil war and fighting.

---

1. Latter Day Saints
2. Napoleon Bonaparte I
3. The barman in the famous Simpsons cartoons

4. Manchester United the famous English soccer team
5. A young boy marooned in Tonga in 1806 who co-wrote the book 'Tonga Islands' which is a first hand account of Tongan society during his 4 years there.

31. POEMS ABOUT GROWNG UP

INNOCENT DAYS

Gone are the innocent days
Of guava, mangoes and tava trays
Bare foot and Sunday 'umu fare
Rugby games, friends to spare

Of lazy hot afternoons
Lying on a treehouse under the moon
Looking over ripe watermelon farms
Peanuts galore and so much fun

Swimming, fishing, falling in love
With every pretty girl, like a dove
Of ten cent movies, five cent peanuts
All night funerals at 40 watts

Church camps and Sunday school
Cheating at marbles, bending the rules
Dreaming of the prettiest girl in town
Clowning when she is around

Of fishing all day at the wharf
Looking up at the King like a dwarf
Hearing tales of New York and London
Where golden streets abound

Playing volleyball with the neighbors
Earning my keep with no labor
When crops and gardens suffice
No need to import rice

Now I learn more
A bit wiser than before
But still a mortal man
Who feels he need to learn

32. POEMS ABOUT FISHING

THE VILLAGE FISHERMAN

He wakes early in the morning
To check his fish traps
And sell some strings for money
School fees, bus fares and bags

His four children are in high school
They dream of a better future
A government job in town
Or become a doctor

But mum says, go overseas
And visit your uncle
Get a job with him
At the shopping mall

They all become cleaners
At Westfield[1] Auckland
Still high achievers
With invested land.

---

1. Westfield is a large shopping mall developer and
    owner in New Zealand.

MANGROVE FISHING

Climb through the maze
Of mangroves before midnight
Pick a good spot for fishing
A branch to sit on

Bait the hook and put it down
Moving it up and down
Until the fishes bite
Then pull up the line

The dead quiet of night
And incoming tide
Bring in the fish to feed

Under the mangroves
Catch a string for the family
To fry or roast on hot coals
Mum and the kids do it
While you have a sleep

Fried or roasted fish
A heavenly taste
For the family
And roaming clucking chicks.

THE OLD FISHERMAN

He stands on the shore everyday
Rain, sunshine, storm, hurricane
His ever present folding net
In his gnarled ancient hands

He watches the incoming tide
Surface movements of the water
Giving away the fish underneath
He knows the species and size

His eyes marked with deep furrows
Skin that has seen better days
His tattered hat and clothes

Gave him the look of a scare-crow

He moves forward quietly, slowly
As the school of fish comes closer
Then in one swift movement
He throws the spreading net

The water surface boils
As the fish tries to escape
Enclosed in nylon fibers
Destined for his family's dinner

He looks up and smiles
A good catch, he says
His bright eyes shining
With a successful day.

NIGHT FISHING

Three men got in a dinghy
And sped away into the night
All fishing gear on board
Baskets for the catch

They reach their spot
As dusk disappear into darkness

Fed their lines into the deep
Hoping fish was present

The lights of the Nuku'alofa waterfront
Look bright and comforting
As they drift through the night
Filling their baskets

Fish were standing in line
To be hauled up one by one
Rock cod, emperor, trevally
Many more before dawn returning

Mum fried the fish for breakfast
A delicious meal every time
For the night-time fisherman
Before he rests.

THE SHELLFISH GATHERER

She plans to feed her family
On shellfish from the reef
No need for credit or money
Corned beef, lamb and noodles

Preparing her bucket
Her knife and old tyre shoes
She ties a scarf on her head

Protection from the cold wind

Then she walks down to the beach
And turned every stone and rock
Until she gets to the deep end
Collections of sea slugs, snails and cockles

Small octopuses run
Disturbed by her shoes
Black ink a dead give away
She collect them too

She finds a new shellfish
A large triangular snail
She heard its a government venture
For seafood collectors

It has become plentiful
On the edge of the reef
A gift from Hikule'o[1]
God of her ancestors

Her family feast that night
On all kinds of seafood she found
The kids grew tall and strong
And the husband is grateful

They do well at school
From all the omega 3
Sent by Tangaroa and Maui
Presents for her fishing skills.

---

1. God of the spirit world in Tongan mythology

33. POEMS ABOUT PACIFIC ISLANDERS

THE ISLANDER

Legends say he comes from Hawaiki
In the mythologies maybe Hawaii
He is white, black or brown
And always has hair on his crown

He is strong and confident
Bright, smiling, his health is excellent
Probably from navigating
The oceans when he is not dating

Fijian, Samoan, Maori, Hawaiian
All islanders by many names
Expert navigators of the ocean
They can sail round the world with no problem

He lives by traditions and cultures
And dances in the night

His love and loyalty
Is to his family

He finds the new world to his liking
It fits his purpose like a dream
Now he flies in a plane
With no canoe to his name.

34. POEMS ABOUT DRINKING AND ALCOHOL

ALCOHOL

Scientists call it ethanol
Kids call it booze
It was banned with only an hour
Of freedom to choose a drink

They pack all the pubs
Cheers and bottoms up
Until everybody is drunk
Or the beers have all run out

It's different now
Drink as much as a cow
Anytime, anywhere
As if you don't care

Is alcohol a problem?
Who created them?
We are not very brave
Driving our kids to the grave

At home I drink six bottles
In a party, I lose the throttle
Consuming everything in sight
Crashed the car and all my rights

The officials changed the age
When I can drink with my mates
But I still drink at home
They won't know, I am all alone

Then they added more tax
I cannot afford a six pack
So I make my own brew
My mates say it's the best booze

I am now 50 years old
And playing my role
To show the kids
Drink more like a chick!

THE BEER DRINKER

I took more out of alcohol

Then it did out of me
Says Winston Churchill
A lover of spirits and beer

Scientists have discovered
Why red wine promotes health
Drink it in small amounts
Anti-oxidants neutralize free-radicals

Beer contain phyto-chemicals
Flavonoids and others from hops
And added plant products
Promote digestion and good cheer

Alcohol in small amounts
Clear the cobwebs in the brain
And tissues, arteries and veins
Drink a few beers a day

If you are scared of pretty girls
Alcohol can help you
Just don't drink too much
Or you'll sound like a goat

Nothing like a cold beer on a hot day
Even better after some hard work
Three cheers for the inventor of beers
Cold freezers and coolers.

COLD BEER

Oh gallon, of beer feeds my desire
I bid thy love drops on my tongue
Cooling thirst in the heat
As the cock crows twice on the beach
Moans of satisfaction
Feeds my imagination
Beam me through time and space
Let's meet in another place

On the planet Tasso
Bring your bag of mussels
And your smiles of bubbles
Champagne to warm our spirits
We become one in body
Fulfilling emotions, dreaming
A gallon of moaning
Shadows and visions fogging.

35. POEMS ABOUT GROWING OLD

GROWING OLD

I need to show my children
The way, where I have been
Where the dangers are
And joys to give

But I find they prefer
To discover and feel the pain
Of misery and disappointment
Because my voice cannot be heard
I am a person of no importance
I need to make lots of money
To prove I am a man
My university degrees don't matter
They cannot imagine how hard I worked
To get where I was
And lost many battles but still win my fights
I need to rein in fame and fortune
From the wisdom of the ages
Shakespeare and Chaucer
Wordsworth, Coleridge and Stevenson
Ancient books still have more wisdom.

INTELLIGENT AMOEBA.

The spermatozoa swam in the dark
Through the womb towards the egg
Fusing, dividing to form a fetus
Another human Prometheus[1]

It grabbed the wall of the womb
And stuck to it like in a tomb
For nine months it grew and rolled
Getting ready in a ball

Then it heard its mother's cry
To move out it must be a sign
Dropping out to suck air
Exhausting as if in despair

First he learned to suck milk
Then cry for everything he needs
He became a little boy
Fascinated with his toys

As a young man
He enjoys the women
Talk, walk, dinner then fight
What's the point of being right

His children calls him Dad
The wife drives him mad
White hairs are on his crown
He left one day and cannot be found

Now he walks with a stick
Teasing his neighbor to show his wit
He does not cry anymore
Although walking make him sore

Then one day he woke up
Beside St Peter with a pup
Welcome to heaven, he said

---

1. Prometheus – From Greek mythology, a Titan who tricked Zeus and stole fire from the Gods to help mankind…he was chained to a rock as punishment and an eagle fed on his liver everyday but grows back overnight. Heracles shot the eagle and set him free.

36. POEMS ABOUT CHARITY

CHURCH CHARITY

I spend nine years
Collecting bread for charity
Every Sunday before some beers
It seems like eternity

Budget organizations estimate
Increases in financial difficulties
Collect bread from your mate
Save money for the family

Queues at the salvation army
Are getting longer
Food parcels disappear quickly
They need food more

Lessons in poverty
Exercises in liberty
It's your own choice
If you have hungry boys.

THE TRUST

A non-profit organization for the poor
Poor in health, spirit, wealth and education
Empowering the grassroots too
Job creation, fighting for a nation

A nation of the down trodden
Like dried mangoes that have not fallen
A sign of things gone wrong
Maybe a disease or master plan

A master-plan of the rich
To drive the poor to the South
Flying cars, shops, brooms like a witch
Nothing but expletives, unintentional slips

A plan to employ our children
Make a dollar and be grateful
Earn two hundred dollars from collections
Sold books, forgotten songs and impressions.

MEN'S REFUGE

There's none in New Zealand
They only care about the women
If the Mrs kick you out
You just have to sleep outside
Under the skies
Covered with flies
No money, No job, No luck
You try your talent with no buck
Just grab your backpack
And leave like a rat
As long as you can eat and sleep
Or hide in a boat among the wheat
Go and see the world
Leave that stupid girl
Your love for the children
Will not matter you'll just get beaten.

37. POEMS ABOUT TECHNOLOGY

BARCODE ECONOMY

Everyone has to have one
Like a tax number and phone
Recording work hours
Pay and shopping spending

A chart for health reminders
The world shares its wealth
With every man, woman and child
No longer billionaires but frugal

All men will have jobs
And some place to live
Enough money for the family
Holidays, medical and drinks

A new world order arrives
With the electronic barcode
In your body where no one can steal
Read by scanners on roads and space

The world government control everything
Where you stay, work and sleep
Where you shop, holiday and drink
No more poverty or rich.

INFORMATION AGE

Books have lost favor
In the information age
Bookshops close from low sales
Internet e-books rise

Read books on your phone
E-book reader or computer
A modern library in cyber space
Cannot replace a book in the hand

One room gone from the house
Where once a collection abound
A place for relaxation and knowledge
Now replaced by a single gadget

Knowledge is not worth a cent
In the information age, it is free
It does not pay to be knowledgeable
Hard labor pays more.

NOTES ABOUT THE AUTHOR.

Semisi Pule also known as Semisi Pule Pone attended Longolongo Primary School (1967-1974) and Tonga High School (1974-1979) in Tonga before attending Mt Albert Grammar School (1980) and the University of Auckland (1981-1984, 1987-1988) in New Zealand. He graduated from the University of Auckland with a Bachelor of Science in 1985 and a Master of Science (Hons) in 1989. He worked for the Ministry of Agriculture, Fisheries and Forests in Tonga, as a research Plant Pathologist and Senior Plant Virologist from June, 1985 to February 1992. During his time in Tonga he was involved with some large projects such as control of the viruses attacking vanilla, kava and squash pumpkin. Tonga exported 22,000 tonnes of squash pumpkin to Japan in 1991 despite the presence of the destructive zucchini yellow mosaic virus (ZYMV).

He was appointed a Fellow at the University of the South Pacific, Samoa, Agriculture Campus; Institute for Research, Extension and Training in Agriculture from March 1992 to May 1993. He did a lot of research in the multiplication of vanilla *in vitro* and long-term storage of sweet potatoes during his time there. This work is already published in PLANT PROTECTION IN THE PACIFIC 3 available from amazon.com

In June 1993 he was appointed the Plant Protection Officer/Advisor and Coordinator for the South Pacific Commission's Plant Protection Service in Suva, Fiji.

He was the Manager for the SPC/EU Pacific Plant Protection Project with a budget of $NZ5 million. The project funded staff, information transfer, plant quarantine, plant protection equipment and training, as well as travel and meetings for the member countries.

He was also the coordinator and assisted many other major projects in Plant Protection with a total budget of more than $NZ30 million.

During his time with SPC he also did some work for the United Nations Food and Agriculture Organization in Global Plant Quarantine Standards and Regional Plant Protection Organizations which met in Rome every 2 years.

His work in Tonga and the South Pacific Commission, Fiji (now known as the Secretariat for the Pacific Community) are already published in PLANT PROTECTION IN THE PACIFIC 1 & 2. Both books are available from amazon.com.

He moved to New Zealand in 1996 and started a business. He also did a lot of other work in the last 18 years. Some of his experiences are written in books and ebooks like "**If you can't find a job start a business**", 'Success' and 'We are all millionaires' with the aim of helping unemployed people with his experience.

He is currently running a business called LAWN AND GARDEN MANAGEMENT and his book writing and publishing business called RAINBOW ENTERPRISES.

As Chief Executive of the Project Revival Charity Trust (Inc) he is responsible for implementing the Trust programmes approved by the Board of Trustees.

He writes children's stories with the series "**The Children of the Gods**" the first one. He also writes humor, poetry, religion, science and novels.

Semisi Pone has more than 100 books and ebooks on sale in New Zealand and worldwide in blurb.com, amazon.com, wheelers.co.nz and apple.com.

DONATION

If you wish to make a donation to help the Trust with its reading programme please contact Semisi Pone, Chief Executive, PRCT, email : rainbowenterprises7@gmail.com Phone: 642102695563.

The Trust aim to print and distribute story books for the kids in Northcote, as Christmas presents, every year. On Christmas 2015, the Trust distributed 60 copies of the DREAMTIME STORIES by Semisi Pone to the kids in Northcote as Christmas presents. The book contain 12 short stories by Semisi Pone on a 120 page gift quality paper back printed from the United States. This was made possible with a $1,000 grant from the Auckland Communities Foundation.

From the first distribution in 2015 we know there are many more kids who would like to be part of the reading programme and receive a book every year. This year (2016) we aim to print 200 books and give them as Christmas presents to our kids and youth in Northcote.

www.ingramcontent.com/pod-product-compliance
Lightning Source LLC
Chambersburg PA
CBHW071957040426
42447CB00009B/1371